Please read this book! For years I have wondered why so many people in our churches believe that they are saved but show no signs of spiritual life. Perhaps it is not that we have denied the gospel but unknowingly reduced it to a "prayer" or "decision" giving people permission to think they are saved even though they have never experienced the conviction of sin that leads to repentance. If what Karl writes is correct—and I think it is—we had better rethink how we lead people to Christ.
Erwin W. Lutzer, Pastor Emeritus, The Moody Church, Chicago

Karl Clauson has hit the nail on the head: Telling people that they are saved when they know nothing of repentance or of new life in the power of the Spirit sets them up to abandon the faith they may think they have embraced but, in reality, have never experienced. Writing in his distinctive high-octane style, and with a passion that compels, Karl brings hope by showing that there is more to the gospel than disappointed and defeated believers have known. This book is a must-read for anyone who is tempted to deconstruct their faith and for all who are tired of a shriveled gospel and are looking for more.
Colin S. Smith, President, Open the Bible; Pastor Emeritus, The Orchard

There is not another man, preacher, husband, father, or pastor that Ann and I respect more than Karl Clauson. His fire for Jesus and for truth is inspiring and contagious. And in this book he is going to take you on a journey to the heart of Jesus and what true salvation looks like and how that salvation leads to true discipleship. The time for this book is so now and the ramifications for the body of Christ will ripple through to the generations coming after us. Study this piece of work and then apply it and watch the fire of the gospel burn a new legacy!
Dave and Ann Wilson, cohosts of *FamilyLife Today*

Today the church finds itself in a dangerous place. In many cases, a growing "easy believism" has replaced the true, radical call of Jesus' gospel. To believe in Christ is no longer laced with repentance, surrender, and a commitment to follow. Now it's "just believe": a half-baked gospel decision that neither frees the heart nor transforms one's life. No one makes this insidious cancer infecting and undermining today's church clearer than my good friend Karl Clauson. Karl's keen insight and deep ministry experience over the years makes him well suited for speaking to our present age about what the true gospel is . . . and isn't. *The Unstoppable Gospel* is a must-read for all of us. I highly recommend it!
Robert Lewis, pastor, founder, BetterMan and Men's Fraternity

Modern Christian culture has so watered down the gospel that it's no longer the gospel. It's a bland, benign feel-good message that leaves many with a false sense

of security. This book needed to be written, and Karl was the one to write it! I pray these words ignite a holy revival in the hearts of many. The church needs this wake-up call!
Susie Larson, bestselling author, national speaker, talk radio host

Karl Clauson nails it right here: "The unstoppable gospel is not just a transformative event. It is a life to be lived." This is why Karl is one of the country's best communicators: He's not a fan of time wasted or punches pulled. There are a thousand "crises" churches are experiencing. But Karl is writing about the crisis that lies below them all: a failure of discipleship.
Brant Hansen, radio host and bestselling author of *Unoffendable* and *The Men We Need*

Karl has named the ache beneath so much of our ministry: We keep trying to disciple people who were never truly born again. With pastoral honesty and four decades of hard-won conviction, he refuses the cheap substitutes and calls us back to a conversion that is genuinely supernatural and a discipleship that is Spirit-empowered, not self-powered. Leaders weary of managing behavior instead of witnessing transformation will find clarity, courage, and hope in these pages.
R. York Moore, President & CEO, Coalition for Christian Outreach, author, speaker, evangelist

I've known and appreciated Karl Clauson for many years, and his heart for Christ and His gospel shines through every page of this book. *The Unstoppable Gospel* is a timely, biblical call to rediscover the life-changing power of the true gospel and the joy of making genuine disciples.
Mark M. Yarbrough, President, Dallas Theological Seminary

Karl Clauson is a convictional Christian leader who writes prophetically: "It's impossible to disciple lost people." His unwavering commitment to the Bible issues a clear call to return to, believe in, and stand on *The Unstoppable Gospel*!
Ronnie W. Floyd, Pastor Emeritus, Cross Church; Former President of the Southern Baptist Convention

Karl Clauson beautifully outlines the discipleship process as a fitting response to God's amazing love and empowered by God's enabling grace (1 Cor. 15:10). May it be a means God uses to revive His people and awaken countless others to experience Christ's merciful salvation for the glory of God.
Bill Thrasher, Professor Emeritus, Moody Bible Institute; author of *How to Resurrect a Dead Prayer Life*

"A diluted gospel inevitably produces diluted discipleship." This caught my attention! Karl takes the reader on an amazing journey of self-reflection. In *The Unstoppable Gospel*, Karl has shared his over forty years of ministry experiences. His uncompromising gospel proclamation is a breath of fresh air in our times of emphasis on methodologies and strategies.
Samuel Naaman, Professor of Intercultural Studies at MBI; VP of Call of Hope

We need to recover the undiluted, uncompromising, unedited, and unchanging gospel of Jesus Christ. Thankfully, Karl Clauson embraces the same conviction, which is why we have his book, *The Unstoppable Gospel*. I'm grateful for his honesty and earnestness, as he calls people to believe and obey "the rugged, transformative gospel of Scripture." Its message is needed today, now more than ever.
Nate Pickowicz, pastor, Harvest Bible Church; author of *Overcoming the Darkness: Biblical Help for Spiritual Depression*

Mere mental assent to the claims of Christianity is not enough. Karl Clauson calls for a return to a robust, New Testament discipleship that involves an intentional, Spirit-filled pursuit of Christ in every area of life. Karl both challenges believers to reject shallow Christianity and demystifies discipleship so that every believer can know, follow, and understand the call to walk worthy of the gospel.
Daniel Darling, director of The Land Center for Cultural Engagement and author of several books, including *The Characters of Christmas*

This is a "must read" for anyone ready to experience the power of real discipleship in their lives and in the lives of those they lead and influence! With grace and humility, Karl challenges and provokes the reader out of comfortable, watered-down Christianity and into a life of sacrifice and surrender: the discipleship Jesus called us to. If you want to follow Jesus at all costs; if you want to be propelled to a life of fire and adventure and accelerated growth in spiritual muscles you didn't even know you had, then this book is for you!
Lana Silk, President and CEO, Transform Iran

With both courage and biblical clarity, *The Unstoppable Gospel* exposes a glaring issue in our day, which is a counterfeit gospel that fills our churches yet leaves hearts unchanged. This book wounds before it heals, but the healing is worth it.
Dr. James Coakley, Professor of Bible, Moody Bible Institute, author, *14 Fresh Ways to Enjoy the Bible*

Maybe instead of encouraging people to invite Jesus into their heart, we should have been emphasizing Jesus inviting them into His heart. Making it easy to

think you are a Christian has made it more complicated to actually be one. You DEFINITELY need to read Karl's book.
Tim Kimmel, author of *Grace Based Parenting*

If you long for the church to be a place that makes genuine disciples and shares a gospel that transforms lives from the inside out, this book is essential reading. It will convict, encourage, and equip you to champion truth and unleash the power of Christ in your life and community.
Shaunti Feldhahn, bestselling author of *For Women Only, For Men Only*, and *When Hurting People Come to Church*

If you love the gospel and the church, read this! If you want to know how to help others fully commit to Christ and embrace Him as Lord, read this. If you want people to know the difference between being "in Christ" and "in church," you need to read Karl's compelling stories and relevant ideas.
Kathy Koch, Founder of Celebrate Kids, Inc.; speaker, podcaster, and an author of nine parenting books including *8 Great Smarts* and *Resolve Conflict and Find Peace and Hope with Adult Children*

What does it profit the church to grow in numbers if many within it remain spiritually lifeless? *The Unstoppable Gospel* offers a timely call to return to Christ through genuine repentance and wholehearted surrender.
Greg Dempster, Founder and Director, ChristLife Ministries

Karl understands and illuminates that "try harder" doesn't work. It's when totally grasping Jesus' radical and revolutionary gospel that we are transformed, changed, surrendered, and yielded, becoming a dedicated disciple of Jesus desirous of modeling and teaching others about His work "in and through" us. Stop settling. Become unstoppable!
Joe and Cindi Ferrini, authors of *The Special Needs Parent: A Guide to the Life You Never Expected*

This book is Karl distilled to his purest conviction. What he names here comes from his heart: We do not simply have a discipleship problem; we have a gospel problem. *The Unstoppable Gospel* is the most honest and courageous treatment of this crisis I have read. Every pastor and church leader I know needs this book.
Drew Dickens, founder of Encountering Peace and host of *The AI & Spirituality Podcast*

THE UNSTOPPABLE GOSPEL

From Powerless Belief to a True Faith That Changes Everything

KARL CLAUSON

Moody Publishers
CHICAGO

Edited by Pamela Joy Pugh
Interior design: Tammy Adelhardt
Cover design: Kaylee Lockenour Dunn

ISBN: 978-0-8024-4124-9

Originally delivered by fleets of horse-drawn wagons, the affordable paperbacks from D. L. Moody's publishing house resourced the church and served everyday people. Now, after more than 125 years of publishing and ministry, Moody Publishers' mission remains the same—even if our delivery systems have changed a bit. For more information on other books (and resources) created from a biblical perspective, go to www.moodypublishers.com or write to:

Moody Publishers
820 N. LaSalle Boulevard
Chicago, IL 60610

1 3 5 7 9 10 8 6 4 2

Printed in the United States of America

To every brokenhearted mom and dad, brother and sister, son and daughter who wants nothing more than those you love to know and follow Jesus.

To those who have struggled to find comfort in church attendance, religious activity, and prayers prayed, yet still long for something more—the unmistakable evidence of a transformed life under the lordship of Christ.

And to every pastor who has come to the painful realization that it is far easier to gather a crowd than to make disciples, and who carries the burden of knowing that many in the church may not yet be in Christ.

If your heart aches for a gospel that is clear about salvation, uncompromising in truth, and powerful enough to produce mature disciples of Christ, I dedicate this book to you.

Contents

Introduction

A GREAT DECEPTION

It's impossible to disciple lost people.

That sounds obvious. Maybe too obvious to even say out loud. But when the church dilutes or neglects the good news, devastation is left in its wake.

After forty years of ministry, this is the most sobering truth I've learned about the Western church: We do not merely have a discipleship problem today. We have a gospel problem. Before we ever became weak at disciple-making, we began redefining conversion itself. We slowly traded supernatural regeneration for human decision. Salvation became a prayer to repeat, a card to sign, an aisle to walk, while millions were assured of heaven without ever being transformed by the power of God. We didn't offer them a belief lacking power, we offered them a powerless belief.

The result is a generation that has been deeply Christianized but not necessarily changed. They know the language. They know the songs. They know when to stand, when to sit, when to say amen. They have been immersed in church culture, yet many have never been brought from death to life. We have filled churches with people who have learned how to function in and around "Christianity" without ever truly following Christ.

And when that happens, discipleship collapses under the weight of human effort. When evangelism centers on human decision, discipleship inevitably becomes self-powered. Following Jesus is reduced to behavior management, moral striving, and "try harder next time." The supernatural life Christ promised is replaced with self-help dressed up in religious garb.

Dallas Willard spoke of "the Great Omission," the church's failure to make disciples. He was right. But I believe something even deeper has happened. Before we omitted discipleship, we compromised the very gospel that births disciples in the first place. That is the crisis. That is the great deception. And until we recover the true faith that changes everything, we will continue trying to disciple people who have never truly been made alive.

A DIFFERENT GOSPEL

I caught my first glimpse of how wide and deep this crisis runs after posting what I thought was a bold but not over-the-top message to social media. It wasn't polished or crafted to perform. It was just a short, straightforward, raw, honest, and urgent post. It scratched the surface of what has become my greatest burden and my greatest hope. It came from a realization that the gospel we preach today often falls short of producing the life Jesus promised. It flowed from a conviction that the church has drifted from the rugged, transformative gospel of Scripture and settled for something softer, safer, and utterly impotent: a different gospel.

I typed it out, hit "post," and went to have lunch. A brief word of context may help here. God has graciously given me opportunities to preach the gospel for more than three decades as a pastor and radio host. Through these platforms, I've had the privilege of speaking to nearly a million listeners each week, walking with people through the joys, failures, heartbreaks, and victories that come with following Jesus. Along the way, I've watched God work in ways that still leave me humbled and amazed.

As an eighteen-year-old, I completed the 1,100-mile Iditarod Trail Sled Dog Race, an experience that taught me early how quickly even grand achievements and self-reliance can leave us empty. My wife and I later lived in South Africa during a season of deep political unrest, helping plant churches and watching the gospel advance in difficult places. Over the years, I've also had the privilege of witnessing powerful movements of prayer and spiritual awakening, including one that fueled the exponential growth of a church in Alaska that reached people from everyday life to leaders in government.

I have seen God's power in ministry that words cannot fully capture, and I have experienced pain that strips away the spiritual veneer. Over time, the number of things I feel certain about has grown smaller, but the truths that remain have only grown deeper. Chief among them is this: Nothing matters more than getting the gospel right. My confidence in raw ability, leadership strategies, and human effort has steadily faded, while my confidence in the power of God has only grown stronger.

And yet, for all of those experiences, one thing remained undeniably true: I was not an online influencer, and nothing I had ever written had come remotely close to going viral. What happened next had nothing to do with branding or marketing instincts. It was simply another reminder that when God chooses to amplify a message, He requires very little from the messenger.

So imagine my surprise when I sat back down at my desk and refreshed the page. Thirty thousand views! A few hours later a hundred and fifty thousand views! Now I'm getting nervous because I don't know what's happening and the reach shocked me. I reread the post to see if something was way out of whack. Nope, just Scripture truth.

By the time I went to bed, I could see it warming up even more. And when I woke up the next morning, it was no longer a slow burn; it was a brushfire, a classic viral post. Four days later, the view count passed 1.1 million. Not record-setting but significant.

Let me be clear: The numbers weren't impressive because they were big—they were impressive because of what they revealed. Something deep in the hearts of God's people resonated with the burden behind that post. Something dormant got stirred. And if a simple, unpolished message could awaken that kind of response, it meant the problem was bigger and far more widespread than even I had imagined.

The comments poured in by the hundreds and the post was shared by thousands. Some questioned my conviction. Others my doctrine. A few laughed it off or mocked it with some colorful language. Many wanted further clarity. But the overwhelming majority responded with a kind of spiritual *aha* as if someone had finally put words to the uneasiness they'd been carrying for years.

Why? Because the truths touched on in that short post were not new. They've been hard truths for at least a couple thousand years. The truths flowed from the deep waters of Paul's letters, particularly to the Galatian church. They echoed Jesus' clear warnings. They confronted the danger of a different gospel that breeds powerless belief and the risk for those who spoke it, a gospel that is unable to change anything. They exposed our cultural reticence to say the word *repentance*, our casual low-bar treatment of salvation, and our failure to equip God's people to preach, pray, and share with compassion or conviction for those who are still far from Him—even though many were raised in church and many more are in church every weekend.

> The greatest danger facing the church today is the deception of salvation.

Underneath all of that ran a deeper truth, one that I've carried for years but have only recently begun to articulate with full weight: The greatest danger facing Christianity today is the false gospel we have offered the world and the church, and the hallucination of salvation people possess—seeing something in themselves that isn't there.

We have, sitting in our church chairs and pews every weekend—even in good, Bible-teaching churches—vast numbers of people who believe themselves to be saved but possess no power beyond their own efforts and whose lives show only surface evidence of new birth. People assume what they have is all God has for them, not knowing they are cultural Christians, so close yet so far from God. People who have been taught a version of Christianity divorced from repentance, from surrender, from the cost of discipleship and, tragically, from the power that makes the gospel unstoppable. Many profess Christ but don't possess Christ.

DILUTED GOSPEL, DILUTED DISCIPLESHIP

And here is the part we rarely admit: This "different gospel" that deceives the lost has deceived even the saved. It has infected our disciple-making–making it thin, hollow, drained of power. We have attempted to build the church on a foundation that cannot save, and so our disciple-making mirrors the message we preach—lightweight, self-willed, activity-heavy, transformation-poor. Well-meaning people are trying harder and getting less. If the gospel that claims to bring someone into the family of God is fraudulent, the formation that follows will be weaker still. A diluted gospel inevitably produces diluted discipleship even among those who are truly saved.

This deception has done more than confuse "Christians." It has truly crippled disciple-making.

You cannot disciple lost people.

You cannot disciple people who have never been born again.

You cannot disciple people who have embraced a gospel that requires nothing of them, confronts nothing in them, and transforms nothing deep within them.

You cannot disciple people, even the truly "born again," who rely more on self-help than emptying themselves of self and finding the grace, patience, and power of God.

And yet this is precisely what we've tried to do for decades.

We've busied our churches with programs, multiplied activities, developed strategies, built facilities, and launched initiatives—yet for all our efforts, the fruit of genuine transformation is increasingly scarce. The numbers don't lie, as you will see. All our efforts and finances have produced little return on investment. And the staggering truth is that the church is drowning in busyness and churchianity while thirsty for life, freedom, and abundance.

We've filled rooms with inspired music but leave them with the same old soundtrack playing in their minds: *I have to make it happen and fake it when it doesn't.* We've baptized children, youth, and adults but left too many hearts deceived and parched. We've told "believing" people they just need another class or more information, while leaving the truth of God's grace (unmerited favor and unparalleled power) untold and unapplied. We have become behavior modifiers and religious pretenders. We have, in the words of Paul writing to Timothy about religious people, a form of godliness but deny its power.

We've left people needing more, wanting more, and settling for too little.

That is why I wrote this book.

My passion in these pages is to pull back the curtain on what has gone wrong, identify the subtle lies we've embraced, and rediscover the rugged, beautiful, unstoppable gospel that still has the power to change everything. I'll identify the "different gospel" that has slithered into our churches—a gospel that is no gospel at all. And you'll understand how we deceived not just one generation, but possibly two or more.

It is not to cause genuine disciples of Christ to question salvation but to reveal and champion what grace has done and provide a great vision of what grace can do. I want us to see how our crippled disciple-making can be restored, strengthened, and unleashed once again.

Before we go any further, let me make two things clear: First, the counterfeit gospel we are about to discuss exists on a continuum. Some have embraced twisted views of the gospel almost completely. Others have recognized the danger and are doing everything they can to fight against it. Most of us fall somewhere in between. But because we live and minister in a culture saturated with nominal Christianity, none of us is untouched by its influence. These are not someone else's challenges. They are our challenges.

Second, early parts of this book may be difficult to read. My aim is not to condemn, discourage, or burden anyone with false guilt. But truth often wounds before it heals. The chapters ahead will expose some hard realities. Stay with me. There is hope on the other side. My goal is not merely to expose the problem, but to recover the beauty, power, and transforming grace of the unstoppable gospel.

But to do that, we must confront the linchpin issue: We must see the spiritual delusion and crisis of humanity for what it is and the cure of God for what He has done. When you truly grasp the depth of human lostness, you stop making broad assumptions and quit trying to convince yourself that those you love are saved, and possibly begin seeing yourself in a revealing light.

You stop looking back at childhood decisions, emotional moments, church involvement, and mission trips to authenticate faith in someone you love and begin to let truth tell their story.

You stop presuming that an emotional experience, a hand raised, or a prayer prayed did something when maybe it did nothing at all. You stop believing that even robust spiritual activity equals spiritual life, and that even a visible position in the church assures no one of eternity with God.

And you begin to see with fresh clarity the breathtaking, undeserved mercy of God that rescues sinners, raises the dead, and produces disciples—not through human effort but through divine power. That is where the hope comes rushing in.

The great deception must end.

There is life for the spiritually dead.

There is reconciliation for those far from God.

There is surrender that leads to life instead of loss.

There is humility that becomes the birthplace of every virtue.

There is repentance that produces the rhythm of a flourishing soul.

There is strength found by embracing and celebrating weakness.

There is discipline that flows from grace instead of fear or performance.

There is introspection that brings clarity to what we cannot see on our own.

And there is deep, liberating, unmistakable freedom when Christ becomes everything.

> The unstoppable gospel does not simply expose what is false. It reveals what is true.

This is why truth must be championed. Not as an idea, but as a reality that cuts, clarifies, and calls us forward. Because when truth becomes really clear, it doesn't just inform you. It changes you. It brings you out of the fog, out of the confusion, out of the illusion—and into a life that is grounded, whole, and fully alive with God.

This is the gospel that birthed the early church. This is the gospel that turned the world upside down. This is the gospel that sustains God's kids under brutal persecution today. This is the gospel the church has forgotten and the good news it desperately needs. This is the gospel that still changes everything today.

I invite you into a journey—a hard line at times, a sobering turn at others—but in the end, an exhilarating and liberating adventure with God. The unstoppable gospel does not simply expose what is false. It reveals what is true. It frees. It awakens. It transforms. And for anyone willing to receive it, it brings resurrection life.

And in the final chapters you'll see how the power God wants to unleash is below the waterline. It's deep, personal, and awe-inspiring. This is the boiler room where the fire is stoked and the power builds. This is the foundation that holds everything else up. The roots that draw life when the surface is dry. The ballast and weight below the waterline that keeps the sailboat upright so the sails can actually capture the wind of the Spirit.

My prayer is simple: that this book would help you see the truth about salvation, the truth about discipleship, and the truth about the gospel that still has the power to change everything.

It is time to stop settling for a powerless belief that is weak, fragile, and hollow. It is time to expose the counterfeit, that different gospel that feels right and quietly settles in as if it were the real thing. And it's time to embrace the cure that heals and become champions of it. And once you do—once you see it—you and those around you will never be the same.

Lead an Unstoppable Gospel Group

Don't walk this journey alone. Gather a small group of people and pursue the kind of faith that changes everything. The leader guide includes an introductory video to show to the group and discussion questions for each chapter, all easily downloadable.

Unstoppablegospel.com/lead

Part One

EXPOSING COUNTERFEITS

Chapter 1

HOW WE DESERTED GOD

I had heard about the "I Believe" services, but I had never seen one. After having recently given two messages at this megachurch, what I was about to experience would put a fresh fire in my belly for the gospel—not from what I witnessed, but what I didn't hear and see.

BLINDER THAN EVER

A few thousand people gathered in that service alone. The music was upbeat and executed with excellence. Before the message, we greeted one other, then everybody took their seats. The message, as I remember, was anecdotal, engaging, and biblically anchored. Everything felt poised for something meaningful.

At the end of the message the worship team took the stage as the pastor gave an invitation. He was offering salvation—to "become a Christian." All anyone needed to do, as the band played softly in the background, was stand where they were and speak out the words, "I believe." Two simple words. That was it.

It started slowly. One here. One there. Then it picked up steam as people seemed to see how relatively simple it was and how many were joining in. Soon, two or three people would be standing and speaking those two words "I believe" at once, from different seats across the auditorium.

Here, "I believe." There, "I believe." Everywhere, "I believe." "I believe." I couldn't get a head count, it was happening so fast, but there must have been seventy people, maybe more, who rose from their seats, said "I believe," and sat back down.

It ended with applause and me sitting alone wondering if anyone else was sick to their stomach. Not because I doubted God's power to save. Not because I thought no one in that room was being drawn by the Spirit. Not because I doubted that God could save someone at that moment. I was sick and sad because I suspected many in that auditorium were now more blinded to their need for God than they were when they walked in.

People arrived lost and some were searching. Many left lost and assured they were saved. A new group of cultural Christians was created that day. One author rightly calls them "the Unsaved Christian."[1] Many of these were still far from God who now believed they had found Him—because they stood for a moment and said, "I believe."

UNBELIEVABLE

I'm on some tender ground here. But I'm pointing the finger at myself and the cultural riptide that has swept pastors, teachers, small group leaders, loving parents, and friends from the rock of truth into a sea of spiritual ambiguity.

We have offered children to "invite Jesus into their heart," led people in "this short prayer," asked people to "come forward," or "raise your hand" while "no one is looking." From honest conversations with sober-minded pastors and testimonies from true disciples who lived in this deception for years and then experienced true faith, what surfaces is this: The vast majority of these evangelistic attempts leave people with false assurance and still lost, with their idols still in place and their lives in pieces.

Yes, there is a belief that saves but what you believe about your spiritual condition and God's provision alone to provide the cure is what changes a life. Mere intellectual assent is a deadly delusion if that's where it stops. Scripture gives us one of the clearest warnings about this kind of empty belief: "You believe that God is one; you do well. Even the demons believe—and shudder!" (James 2:19). Demons believe many other rich truths:

- Demons believe Jesus is the Son of God. (Matt. 8:29)
- Demons believe Jesus is holy. (Mark 1:24)
- Demons believe Jesus has absolute authority over them. (Luke 8:31)
- Demons believe there will be a final judgment and that Jesus will be their Judge. (Matt. 8:29)
- Demons believe they are ultimately doomed. (James 2:19)

Cognitive belief is mere mental assent—agreement with facts about God that never penetrates the will or transforms the life. That kind of belief is orthodox, informed, and even emotionally stirred, yet remains unchanged at the level of allegiance.

By contrast, the saving belief Jesus speaks of is not simply knowing the truth but entrusting oneself to Him, a belief that joins *with* Christ, abides *in* Christ, and inevitably bears fruit through repentance, obedience, and perseverance (John 3:16; 6:35; 8:31). This distinction is crucial because collapsing saving faith into mere cognition produces false assurance—people who "believe" the right things yet remain unregenerate—whereas Jesus consistently ties true faith to a reoriented life, not as a work added to belief, but as the evidence that belief has moved from the mind to the heart and will.

Levels of belief of this sort, as demons have, are not vacant of correct doctrine and undeniable knowledge. And yet they can remain prideful, self-willed, lost, and eternally separated and condemned by God. Demons' belief is real, but it is not regenerative. It is intellectual but not transformational. Demonic levels of belief are widespread in cultural Christianity.

That Sunday morning, as person after person stood and quietly declared "I believe," I realized with grief that many were being offered a belief demons possess—a belief without repentance, surrender, rebirth, transformation, or hope.

That is the tragedy. Not that people responded, but that the response they were called to was impotent and disconnected from the gospel that raises the dead to life.

What if the greatest danger is not the counterfeit you can see—but the one you can't? The kind that sounds and feels right, and quietly settles in as if it were the real thing.

And what if this isn't just about you—but about the people you love most? Your spouse. Your kids. Your friends. The men and women you worship beside every week. And you may no longer be in church because the gospel you embraced in your youth didn't work. But what if it's because it couldn't?

When belief is offered without an invitation to consider the weight of our sin, the call to faith, surrender, and repentance, and without the vision of the cross and the empty tomb, people are not helped; they are harmed, many for eternity.

DECISIONISM

Before we look at Paul's stinging rebuke to those who share "a different gospel," we must confront a quiet but powerful force shaping our churches today: Decisionism.

Decisionism began roughly 250 years ago. During the Great Awakenings a shift happened from divine act to a human response.[2] Its cultural rise emerged out of revival movements where pastors and evangelists, driven by genuine desire to see people saved, developed methods that produced immediate, visible responses. Emotional appeals. Public invitations. "Come forward" moments. Decisionism is pervasive today and impacts us all.

> What began as an evangelistic tool subtly became a theological assumption: The decision itself equals salvation.

Decisionism slid the focus to human will of what we commonly see today—raising a hand, repeating a prayer, walking an aisle, signing a card, whispering a phrase, or standing and saying, "I believe"—rather than by God's regenerating grace producing repentance, faith, and new life in Christ. It is the idea that conversion is something we initiate rather than something God accomplishes by His sovereign will and power.

Over time, what began as an evangelistic tool subtly became a theological assumption: The decision itself equals salvation. Martyn Lloyd-Jones spoke up strongly: "There is no such thing as a decision for Christ. The Christian is one who is born again. The emphasis in the New Testament is not on what we decide, but on what God does."[3]

Decision moments have become the reflexive response when people lack assurance of salvation, when parents are concerned for children who now show no real interest in following Christ, when friends drift far away from God, or when we ourselves look inward and quietly ask, "Am I truly born again?" Decisionism whispers, "Remember the moment. Remember the decision. Remember when you prayed the prayer."

There is a biblical model of public response that flows from repentance (such as Peter's sermon on Pentecost in Acts 2), but the personal cost attached to their confession was high. There are also present-day calls for public response that are healthy and handled responsibly. Take Billy Graham and others like him: the invitation centered on coming to grips with your sin, with clear calls to repentance and surrendering all you are to Jesus. Graham's team was fully equipped with trained counselors who brought biblical clarity about what true faith is.

But consider the profound cost to confessing Christ in the early church and in the persecuted church of today. Compare that with the pervasive cultural Christianity that thrives where there is little cost linked to the decision. Looking back to a point of decision rather than to the robust, present-tense life found in Christ's presence is truly deceptive and dangerous.

Dallas Willard, the father of modern spiritual formation, captured the crisis with piercing clarity: "For at least several decades the churches of the Western world have not made discipleship a condition of being a Christian. One is not required to be, or to intend to be, a disciple in order to become a Christian, and one may remain a Christian without any signs of progress toward or in discipleship."[4] Willard critiques what he calls "the gospel of sin management," defined as "the good news that your sins can be forgiven and you can go to heaven when you die," arguing instead that the gospel is aimed at the "transformation of life and character."[5] And this sin management or behavior modification has left us with a man-centered gospel not tasting and seeing how good God is in the slightest.

> Decisionism separates what Scripture never divides: genuine salvation and complete surrender.

Decisionism is not dangerous because belief is wrong. Transformative belief is awe-inspiring. The power of the gospel is almost indescribable and must be experienced to be understood. But saving belief is never disconnected from repentance, surrender, obedience, and new birth. What turns people from darkness to light is not a surface affirmation or even deep emotion, but the supernatural grace of God invading human brokenness. This is why repentance remains one of the greatest pieces of evidence of genuine faith: Repentance is the first fruit of grace.

Decisionism is still debated. In the 1980s, a dispute erupted over "Lordship salvation." The question was simple: Can someone truly call Jesus Savior while not calling Him Lord? Meaning—can Jesus save your life without ruling your life? A. W. Tozer had spoken to this very issue years before: "The Lord will not save those whom He cannot command. He will not divide His offices. You cannot believe on a half-Christ. We take Him for what He is—the anointed Saviour and Lord. . . . He would not be who He is if He saved us and called us and chose us without the understanding that He can also guide and control our lives."[6] At the end of the day, decisionism separates what Scripture never divides: genuine salvation and complete surrender. It is my deep belief that decisionism has become co-opted by forces of darkness. We have, mostly unknowingly, deceived many who believe they have received all God has to offer while living as the walking dead.

The unstoppable gospel is not just a transformative event. It is a life to be lived. And the assurance of salvation is never found by reaching back to a moment when we stood and said, "I believe," or prayed a prayer, or "invited Jesus into our heart." True assurance is found in the present work of God, in the ongoing evidence that He is sustaining, transforming, convicting, empowering, and growing us. Far from perfection but desperate for His presence.

A DIFFERENT GOSPEL

When Paul wrote to the Galatians, he did not lead off with gentle correction. He wrote frankly, "I am astonished that you are so quickly deserting him who called you in the grace of Christ and are turning to a different gospel" (Gal. 1:6).

This a brutal takedown of twisted teaching and truth with a twist at the end that's a lie. Deserting is a military term—transferring allegiance, defecting to the other side. Paul does not accuse them of abandoning doctrine alone. He accuses them of abandoning God Himself: "deserting him who called you."

A different gospel is not another version. Paul adds, "not that there is another one" (Gal. 1:7). There is no alternative. A different gospel is no gospel at all. And history shows this problem wasn't limited to Galatia. Consider the following:

- Some teachers in Corinth appeared solid but spoke a twisted gospel—and Paul accused them of putting up with that easily. (2 Cor. 11:3–4, 13–15)
- Paul warned of teachers who distorted the gospel to feed their own appetites, whatever those appetites were—glory, influence, status, or self-promotion. (Rom. 16:17–18)
- Jesus warned that some teachers would slam the doors of heaven in people's faces—their teaching shut out God and left their listeners in the dark. (Matt. 23:13–15)
- Paul warned elders that from among their own number—not outsiders—men would arise speaking "twisted things." (Acts 20:26–31)
- Peter warned about destructive heresies that would secretly enter the church and lead many astray. (2 Peter 2:1–3)
- Distorted truth would lead some to depart the faith entirely. (1 Tim. 4:1–2)
- Paul warned Titus that some teachers profess to know God, but deny Him by their lives. (Titus 1:16)

One commonly missed warning is found in John 10. The "thief" in the context of Jesus' teaching is not Satan but false teachers—those who would steal from them the truth, kill them on the altar of rule-following, and destroy their souls. Satan is undoubtedly pulling the levers and is trying constantly to rip us off, but in context, false teachers are responsible for robbing their listeners of finding "life and have it to the full" (John 10:1–10 NIV).

Across Scripture, Old and New Testament alike, the evidence is clear: The message of salvation is constantly at risk of distortion—sometimes intentionally, sometimes negligently, always disastrously.

LET THEM BE ACCURSED

Paul saves the strongest language in his writings for gospel distortion: "But even if we or an angel from heaven should preach to you a gospel contrary to the one we preached to you, let him be accursed" (Gal. 1:8).

Accursed does not mean Paul wants false teachers condemned by his own judgment. It means he appeals to God to deal with those who corrupt the gospel. John Calvin said, "Paul does not accuse them of having renounced Christ openly, but because they had corrupted the purity of the gospel, he declares that they had revolted from God."[7] John Stott agreed:

> To tamper with the gospel is not to reform it, but to destroy it. And to turn from the gospel is to turn from God Himself, for God and the gospel belong together.[8]

A diluted gospel does not save. A partial gospel cannot cause rebirth. A therapeutic gospel produces unconverted churches—filled with people who believe they are saved, still searching for or wondering where there is more, but have never experienced the new birth miracle. This is the crisis we face today. This is why disciple-making has become so crippled. This is why the Western and global church has hundreds of millions who profess faith but do not possess Christ.

Recently, I had just finished sharing the good news of true faith on my radio show. I was clear with what the gospel was all about—God's cure for our condition. I soon received a message that moved me deeply from a listener named Tim. He's seventy-seven years old and has been tuning in to Moody Radio since 1977. What he shared is something I won't soon forget. Here's part of his note:

> After many, many years of having a "new life in Jesus," I found Jesus through your program this morning. I thought I was saved back in 1977, but after a few minutes I realized I was actually saved this morning. I have a joy unspeakable welling up to eternal life! And thanks to you guys, I have eternal life.

When I read that, I teared up, because moments like this remind me what the influence of radio, clear preaching, or having a truth-filled conversation over a cup of coffee with a hurting friend can do. Or a sweet moment of opportunity with a contrite child. It showed me that the power of the Spirit can take truth and pierce hearts, and that's just what the unstoppable gospel is still doing today.

This is a tough truth to embrace. It takes courage to consider that a son or daughter you love, many well-meaning people in your church, a spouse, religious leaders, or even yourself may have never been truly born again. But this is not the end of the story, and this is not a time for despair or self-condemnation; it is a call to rediscover the rugged, beautiful, unstoppable gospel that still has the power to change everything. These truths will equip you to pray rightly and share the hope of Christ with compassion and clarity. Too many lives are at stake to settle for less.

21 Powerful Truths You Can Believe–and Still Not Be Born Again

Belief matters. But Scripture repeatedly confronts us with a sobering reality: a person can possess accurate knowledge, sincere conviction, religious enthusiasm, and even extraordinary spiritual experiences and still not be born again. Read this article to grapple with these truths and learn how true faith responds to each.

Unstoppablegospel.com/believe

Chapter 2

HOW WE DECEIVED A GENERATION

I had nearly a thousand feet of descent in front of me as I dropped out of the Blueberry Hills toward the Norton Sound coast of Alaska. I was roughly 750 miles into the Iditarod Trail Sled Dog Race. My team was running strong but, like me, they were looking for the next village.

SEEING WHAT ISN'T THERE

Sleep deprivation does things to your mind that you don't fully understand until you experience it yourself. I was desperate to reach the next checkpoint: Shaktoolik. I knew what was waiting there—food for my dogs, rest for them before the long push toward Nome, something warm in my stomach, and maybe a couple hours of sleep.

As I descended from Blueberry Hills, the trail flattened out and stretched along the coast. Cold. Windy. Straight. Mushers talk about that stretch as one that always feels longer than it actually is.

Then I saw it. On the horizon, Shaktoolik came into view. As my team trotted closer, the details sharpened. Homes. A few lights glowing. Smoke rising from a chimney. A man outside chopping wood. Relief washed over me. I had made it.

I was already thinking ahead—where I would check in, where the dogs would bed down, how quickly I could get the team fed and grab a wink of sleep. I spotted a home just off the trail with a light on and decided to stop and ask where the checkpoint official was located. I stepped on the brake and pulled my team to a stop, drove my snow hook into the frozen trail, and stepped away from the sled toward the small house.

In a nanosecond, it vanished. The village disappeared completely. Not dimmed. Not blurred. Gone. What sprawled before me now was a vast, empty nothing—wind, frozen ground, and darkness stretching endlessly.

I had heard about hallucinations in endurance racing, but this was my first experience of one, and it was unmistakable. The real village of Shaktoolik was still miles down the trail.

I walked back to my sled discouraged and humbled. What I wanted to see, what I believed I saw, what felt real to me—wasn't real at all. That moment gave me a sobering spiritual perspective I've never forgotten.

Jesus gives us this same strong warning. At great cost, many today are hallucinating spiritually. They think they see something in themselves that isn't real and isn't there.

In Matthew 7, Jesus issues one of the most terrifying warnings in all of Scripture. He tells us that many—not a few—will stand before Him at the moment of judgment, convinced they belong to Him. They will call Him "Lord." They will appeal to ministry involvement and religious activity. And He will say to them, "I never knew you; depart from me."

This is not ignorance; it isn't rebellion. This is deception at the deepest level. It is seeing something in yourself that is not actually there. Jesus places this warning immediately after His teaching on false prophets—those who twist truth just enough to make it believable. Twisted truth is far more dangerous than outright lies because it carries familiar language while emptying it of power and enticing us to embrace powerless belief.

And the impact, Jesus says, will be widespread. Many! Not the openly rebellious. Not those knowingly far from God. But those who believe they know God and that He knows them. People who are religiously active but spiritually dead. This is spiritual hallucination—seeing something in themselves that isn't there.

It is the most dangerous form of deception because it feels settled. It reassures. It quiets the conscience. It convinces people they are safe when they are still miles from the destination—but there is no more trail. Time has run out.

CHRISTIAN IN NAME ONLY

What Jesus warned about in Matthew 7 is no longer just a theological concern—it is now a measurable reality. The most recent Barna research found that 76 percent of people in America call themselves "Christian."[1] According to Pew Research, roughly 24 percent of Americans identify themselves as evangelical Christians.[2] Yet when those same Americans are examined for a worldview that actually orders their private and public lives around the teachings of Scripture, the number collapses. Barna Research reports that only about 4 percent of American adults possess a biblical worldview.[3] The gap between "Christian in name only" and those who order their lives as disciples of Christ is staggering.

It tells us that millions of people profess Christ without possessing a Christian worldview and the passion to live it out. The name remains, but the substance is missing. Identity is disconnected from reality.

It's important to note the solution is not about more church involvement, more knowledge, or reaching moral perfection. It is about new birth—and "many" are simply not born again, though they believe they are.

Jesus made that unmistakably clear when He spoke to Nicodemus, a man who was deeply religious, morally upright, and theologically trained: "Truly, truly, I say to you, unless one is born again he cannot see the kingdom of God" (John 3:3).

The apostle Paul challenged those in the church to presume nothing: "Examine yourselves, to see whether you are in the faith. Test yourselves" (2 Cor. 13:5). That command only makes sense if self-deception is possible.

Paul warned Titus about people fluent in religious language but empty of transformation: "They profess to know God, but they deny Him by their works. They are detestable, disobedient, unfit for any good work" (Titus 1:6).

> Looking ready is not the same as being ready.

The writer of Hebrews spoke to those believing to be inside the covenant community: "Take care, brothers, lest there be in any of you an evil, unbelieving heart, leading you to fall away from the living God" (Heb. 3:12).

James dismantled the illusion of faith without fruit: "So also faith by itself, if it does not have works, is dead" (James 2:17).

Jesus Himself described the final judgment, where people are stunned to discover that casual confidence is not the same thing as relational preparedness. Matthew 25 shatters the illusion that *looking ready* is the same as *being ready*. Five were ready. Five were not. The five foolish bridesmaids carried lamps—religious form, spiritual vocabulary, the appearance of preparation—but no oil, quietly assuming they had what they needed. That assumption is the danger: a subconscious belief that readiness can be determined by external things. But the door closes without warning. The cry comes at midnight, not dawn. And when time runs out, regret and last-minute scrambling are powerless substitutes for a life truly prepared. The parable is a warning to every soul living on borrowed time: You don't drift into readiness—you either have oil or you don't.

These warnings are not aimed at atheists or directed to those openly hostile to God. They are written to people who believe they belong to Him.

And the externality of false spirituality was and is a real problem. Jesus spoke to the indistinguishability between the wheat and weeds and told His disciples that He would sort them out at the final judgment because the external appearance was so similar they may uproot authentic people of faith if they try to separate them now. "Let both grow together until the harvest, and at harvest time I will tell the reapers, 'Gather the weeds first and bind them in bundles to be burned, but gather the wheat into my barn'" (Matt. 13:30).

"Christian in name only" is not a convenient insult. It is a biblical diagnosis. It describes people who are badly mistaken—who are convinced they have arrived while the true destination is still miles down the trail.

HALLUCINATION OF SALVATION

In the relative absence of persecution and in the comfort of cultural Christianity, we have developed a brand of evangelism shaped more by convenience than by depth of conviction, more by decisions than by discipleship. Out of that soil grew what I can only describe as a hallucination of salvation, that is, assurance without repentance, style without substance, Christ believed without Christ followed. Tragically, this was not something we merely practice at home in the Western church. We've exported it. "Christian in name only has gone global."

That reality struck me with fresh force during a conversation with Isaiah, a dear brother and friend, a gospel leader in Burundi. This country is widely regarded as one of the poorest in the world, with an average annual income of roughly $250 per person. It is a place marked by scarcity and suffering.

As I poured out my heart and explained to Isaiah about the deception we are facing in the West, he stopped me. "Karl," he said, "this is our problem too."

That sentence left us staring in silence at each other. Isaiah gathered himself and went on to explain that the same tactics and shallow assurances had taken root there as well. In places where persecution is light or intermittent, pastors had adopted Western methods—quick professions, rousing altar calls, minimal instruction, and little emphasis on repentance, holiness, or the cost of following Christ.

What stunned me most was his clarity. He didn't say they were in danger of doing this. "We are doing this here," he said. "We are leaving people with this great deception you speak of."

His fear was that the church would continue multiplying people who believed they were alive when they were still dead.

When I returned home he urged me to shoot a video for a pastors' conference of several hundred attendees and send it to him so he could share this biblical caution. His fear was not that the gospel would fail. His fear was that the church would continue multiplying people who believed they were alive when they were still dead.

That conversation shattered any illusion that this was merely a Western problem. When a diluted gospel is exported, it does not simply stay diluted—it reproduces dilution and impotence. And when assurance is given without soul transformation, the damage is not local. It is global.

God in His mercy still saves. He always has. He works in spite of us more than because of us. But we dare not presume upon that mercy by continuing to proclaim a gospel that promises so much and asks for so little.

SO CLOSE YET SO FAR

The picture Jesus paints of an eternity separated from God is not abstract. It is deliberate and sobering. When Jesus spoke of hell—or, originally, Gehenna—He was speaking of a real place, one already saturated with judgment, blood, and covenant betrayal.

Jesus Himself teaches that there are degrees of consequence in eternity—gradationalism, or graded judgment. When confronting cities that had witnessed His miracles and still refused to repent, He said, "It will be more bearable on the day of judgment for Tyre and Sidon than for you" (Matt. 11:22).

The severity of judgment, Jesus makes clear, corresponds to gospel exposure resisted and grace refused. Those who saw more of God's works, heard more of God's truth, and stood closer to God's grace are held more accountable for their response.

Eternity is not judged arbitrarily; it is measured by revelation received and resisted.

Here is the reality Jesus intends us to see: The Valley of Hinnom (Gehenna) lies only a few hundred feet from the City of God, Jerusalem. One glance could take in both. The temple. The sacrifices. The songs of ascent. And just beyond the walls, the valley of fire, child sacrifice, divine curse.

Jesus is making a devastating point. He is saying it is possible—especially for those who think they are close to God—to be near the truth, familiar with the language of faith, surrounded by the symbols of worship, and yet be profoundly and eternally lost in a place of horror and separation. These warnings are not aimed primarily at overt rebels or obvious atheists. They are directed toward those who claim the name of God, who live within sight of the city, who assume proximity equals belonging.

Jesus is exposing the danger of nearness without new birth, religion without repentance, familiarity without faith. So close. Yet so far. And with a devastating destiny.

Gehenna stands as the final, haunting image: a warning that proximity to holy things does not equal reconciliation with a holy God—and that the greatest danger is not distance from truth, but the illusion that closeness is enough.

WORDS MATTER

In 1986, seven astronauts stepped into the space shuttle *Challenger* on what was supposed to be a routine mission. Seventy-three seconds after liftoff, the shuttle disintegrated in midair, killing everyone on board. The tragedy was avoidable, but miscommunication and the suppression of truth doomed seven lives.

Engineers had warned that the rubber O-rings sealing the solid rocket boosters become brittle in cold temperatures. The night before launch, they explicitly recommended not launching. But NASA managers pushed back. During a closed-door caucus, those concerns were reframed. One executive told an engineer to "take off your engineering hat and put on your management hat." Management didn't want to hear the truth.

Richard Feynman wrote in the appendix of the Rogers Commission Report, "For a successful technology, reality must take precedence over public relations, for nature cannot be fooled."[4] Seven people were vaporized in an instant.

We have a public relations problem in the greater church culture. Those who have managed the church have broadly suppressed the truth. And the desire to skirt the hard truth for whatever reason has deadly consequences. Most of those reasons are really well meaning, but words matter. They matter when warnings are muted about the space shuttle's operational condition. And they matter most when truth is muted about people's spiritual condition.

I once hosted a radio segment where a man texted in with a comment that still grips me. He said he had finally come into an authentic relationship with Jesus Christ after many years of attending church, and then added this simple line: "I got some bad information." For years, he believed he was fine with God. He wasn't overtly rebellious or hostile to God. He was misled by a church culture and pastors who were unclear with the gospel.

> We have taken sacred realities and replaced them with slogans, formulas, and responses.

When we miscommunicate the gospel—even with good intentions—we don't merely confuse people. We mislead souls. We manage perception instead of proclaiming truth. We hand out assurance where Scripture calls for examination. And the cost is not theoretical. The cost is eternal.

What I'm about to say is really hard for some to hear but don't let conviction turn into condemnation! Today is a new day and God can cleanse us from anything we may have unknowingly messed up in the past. But here is the plain truth: Far too many of the words we've taught people to say and the actions we've encouraged people to do have been treated as if they will certainly lead to salvation. Many of these tactics and phrases have led to deep hallucinatory deception.

Some of them may be used by God as a doorway into genuine faith. God can supercharge a sentence. He can use a stumbling prayer and meet someone in a moment of brokenness. But most of these phrases, as we commonly use them, are dangerously thin and have led to people dying while still "dead in their trespasses and sins."

We have told people to respond with words and actions like:

- "Ask Jesus into your heart"—Jesus never instructs this, and it is nowhere found in the New Testament. Many have essentially invited Jesus to cohabitate with other gods of the age.
- "Accept Jesus"—Many have accepted Jesus, but only those who *receive* Him are called children of God. We accept many things in life without surrendering to them and embracing them, and the same can happen with God.
- "Make Jesus your personal Savior"—Aside from the reality that we cannot make salvation happen, Jesus can only be Savior where He is first Lord of every square inch of who we are and what we become.
- "Pray this prayer"—There is no single prescribed prayer for salvation. Salvation is a cry of the soul. All we can offer is our heart's cry and desperate need for a Savior, surrendering all we are to Christ. Many words can be repeated without regenerating a heart.
- Say "I believe"—The problem is that "even the demons believe—and tremble." Mental assent to Christ's deity without repentance and obedience leaves people with a shallow hallucination. They believe, but it costs nothing and changes nothing.
- "Walk the aisle and come forward"—Many have stepped out in an emotional moment but have yet to follow Jesus Christ. Pressure to move physically can lead to a false eternal security if not fully explained why they are walking and who they are following.

We have taken sacred realities—repentance, faith, reconciliation with God, union with Christ—and replaced them with slogans, formulas, and responses that fail to communicate the curse of sin or the cure of the cross.

The New Testament speaks of new birth. New creation. Repentance and faith. A life that bears fruit. A Savior who does not merely add Himself to your life but becomes Lord, Master, and Ruler of it.

When the gospel is blurred, people don't simply walk away confused—they remain blind.

If we tell someone they are saved because they repeated words but have never trusted in Christ alone, never turned to follow Christ, and remain unchanged and unregenerated, then we have not helped them. We have potentially inoculated them against the very gospel that could save them. They are anesthetized to the reality of their spiritual condition.

This battle over clarity is ancient. Words matter. Paul understood this, which is why he wrote, "We refuse to practice cunning or to tamper with God's word, but by the open statement of the truth we would commend ourselves to everyone's conscience in the sight of God" (2 Cor. 4:2).

To tamper means to alter, to reshape the message so it feels more acceptable. Paul contrasts this with an open statement of the truth—plain, unvarnished clarity. He explains why it matters: "And even if our gospel is veiled, it is veiled to those who are perishing" (v. 3). Here's a hard truth that pastors, leaders, and evangelists have got to embrace as a real threat to themselves and their hearers: A misplaced need to be seen as effective and proficient can be a subconscious driver that leads us to compromise truth on the altar of success.

When the gospel is blurred, people don't simply walk away confused—they remain blind.

WE WERE WARNED

These "decisionism" actions are not new. Respected voices have warned for over two hundred years that reducing conversion to a decision would produce false assurance.

Charles Spurgeon said, "I fear that many have a faith which is no faith at all, a repentance which needs to be repented of, and a hope which is no hope, but a delusion."[5]

J. C. Ryle warned, "It is vain to suppose that we are Christians, if we are not converted."[6]

Jonathan Edwards cautioned against mistaking intense emotion for true conversion during the Great Awakening: "There are such things as false religious affections."[7]

Dietrich Bonhoeffer warned of cheap grace, which is "grace without discipleship, grace without the cross, grace without Jesus Christ, living and incarnate."[8]

Martyn Lloyd-Jones said, "A sinner is not saved because he makes a decision. He is saved because God has regenerated him."[9]

Dallas Willard wrote, "The idea that you can trust Christ and not intend to obey him is an illusion." And also, "You can no more trust Jesus and not intend to obey him than you could trust your doctor and not follow his advice."[10]

Across centuries. Across cultures. Across denominations. We were warned.

Scripture reserves its strongest warnings for those who teach: "Not many of you should become teachers, my brothers, for you know that we who teach will be judged with greater strictness" (James 3:1). And again: "If anyone is preaching to you a gospel contrary to the one you received, let him be accursed" (Gal. 1:9). We were warned.

The tragedy is that this twisted gospel—which is no gospel at all—has been repeated for so long that it no longer comes from a few voices. It has been absorbed into the broader Christian culture itself. Most of us have celebrated cheap grace at some level. We've used the same deceiving words ourselves, wanting the best for those we love and lead and settling for less.

For a variety of reasons we simplified the gospel until clarity was lost. Over time, these miscommunications became familiar. Normal. Expected.

We celebrate children and adults who stake claim to a faith they may not possess. The result is a culture filled with people who are confident they are saved, yet untouched by the transforming power of God. And that is how a generation can be deceived—not by denying the gospel, but by diluting it.

Two truths are needed right now for protection from Satan who wants to accuse and discourage you:

1. God works in spite of us and it's He alone who saves our spouses, our children, our parents, our friends, and even those at church who may be far from God.
2. Our work is to communicate the gospel clearly and pray according to what is most evident. Being honest with ourselves about ourselves or where others are with God may bring some initial sadness. But it is freeing to have personal assurance and pray for those we love to one day know that they stand with God and He stands with them.

Stories of Deception

Spiritual deception is a real threat to the souls of people. We can see things in ourselves that aren't there, including salvation. Watch three people share their stories that reveal how people can believe they are saved while living under a dangerous hallucination of salvation and how God changed everything.

Unstoppablegospel.com/deceived

Chapter 3

HOW WE CRIPPLED DISCIPLE-MAKING

Some assumptions are incredibly dangerous. When I was fifteen, my friend Calvin and I took our dog teams into Alaska's backcountry for an overnight trip to Trout Lake Cabin on the Resurrection Pass Trail. We were too young to drive, so we recruited our friend Dave, a man in his early thirties. He knew just a bit about the outdoors but was willing to come because he was the only one old enough to drive the dog truck. Calvin and Dave rode together on one sled, while I drove my own five-dog team. With camping gear weighing down our sleds and more than a thousand feet of climbing ahead of us, the nearly eight-mile trip pushed our dogs to the edge of what they had ever done.

The night was brutally cold. We ran alongside the sleds to help the teams on the climb, sweating in the subzero air and then cooling quickly whenever we stopped. After a few hours, we spotted a cabin in the trees. Relief washed over us. Certain we had arrived, we pulled in and hurried to our shelter.

Our relief vanished instantly. Our headlamps revealed that every window was shattered. The door had been kicked in. Snow had drifted deep inside, burying the stove and covering rusted bunks stripped down to bare springs. We lit a small Optimus stove, made some toast, and tried to warm ourselves, but it was obvious we could not stay. The dogs were exhausted and hungry. We were cold and worn down, but did not have a place to stay. So we turned around and headed back to the truck, assuming we had reached Trout Lake Cabin without a second thought.

Only the next day did we learn the truth. The structure where we had stopped was not Trout Lake Cabin. It was an abandoned trapper's cabin. The warm, fully stocked Forest Service cabin we had reserved was less than half a mile farther down the trail. We had come all that way and turned back just short of the very thing we were looking for.

That story illustrates a tough point because it captures how dangerous assumptions can be, not only in the wilderness but in every aspect of life. Some assumptions about how we're doing spiritually could leave us out in the cold, thinking we've arrived, feeling something is not right, but coming up short of God's will.

COMING UP SHORT

Churches in the West and beyond have adopted assumptions that come up short. For decades, we have counted noses and nickels as the primary metric of whether we have arrived. How many people showed up and how much money came in. These are not bad metrics. Attendance matters. Giving matters. The book of Acts itself records how many were added to the church. God is not embarrassed by growth, and neither should we be. The story of Acts is church expansion and growth and should be celebrated.

The problem isn't that we measure how many are coming or how much money is given. The danger is that we stop there, and then quietly begin validating or, sadly, invalidating ourselves by those numbers. When a pastor or engaged church members are asked how their church is doing, the usual response is to cite attendance and giving trends—more is good, less is bad. When nickels and noses become the scoreboard, something subtle but deadly happens. We begin to confuse activity with transformation, crowds with conviction, momentum with maturity. It can be very intoxicating.

But none of those numbers, by themselves, answer the most important question we could ask: Are we making disciples? A crowded auditorium can look like success. A growing budget can feel like validation. Even counting salvations and baptisms can create the impression that lives are being discipled and transformed. But appearances can deceive.

When we measure the wrong things, we can make the assumption that all is well while people remain unsaved or un-discipled. This may be the most dangerous assumption the modern church has ever made.

THE COST OF DISCIPLESHIP

Scripture celebrates numbers, yes—but look more closely at what those numbers represented; not casual attendees or spiritual consumers. Early church numbers represented a price that was paid. These were men and women who repented publicly, were baptized immediately, and then often had to walk away or were driven away from family relations, cultural identity, religious tradition, and real social security. Many were cut off from every earthly relationship except those found in Christ. Following Jesus didn't add a compartment to their lives; it reordered everything.

Discipleship is costly in parts of the world today, but the church is thriving in the face of persecution. Tobin Perry from Global Christian Relief reports that Nigeria, China, India, and Indonesia are the top four countries where Christianity is growing the fastest per capita in the world today.[1] The one thing these four countries have in common is intense or growing persecution. Other reports say Iran and Afghanistan are at the top of that list but because of fierce persecution the numbers are hard to verify. It appears that the cost of discipleship has not prevented growth and freedom in Christ but actually somehow cultivates and propels discipleship of courageous followers of Christ.

A quick look at the numbers Luke celebrates in Acts on the day of Pentecost demonstrates that these decisions came with a cost. Thousands of people who died to their old lives and stepped into a new life, gave up everything they had relied on, which could possibly cost them their lives. They knew it but they followed Jesus no matter the cost.

Consider this. Could it be that primarily measuring attendance and giving has weakened us and in turn crippled disciple-making? We often count people who have added Jesus without ever asking whether they have surrendered to Him. We count seats filled without asking whether hearts have been changed and not having a clear strategy to do something about it.

When the wrong metrics lead to false assumptions, the church may look successful while quietly drifting from the very thing that will spin the flywheel of spiritual momentum: disciples making disciples. In our pursuit of numerical growth and financial sustainability, we took our eyes off Jesus' actual commission to "go and make disciples." Could it be that focusing again on the great commission of disciple-making would breathe fresh wind of the Holy Spirit into our houses of worship again?

A NEW (OLD) WAY

Christianity, as it exists for many in the West, is a remarkably good gig. It costs little and disrupts almost nothing. This version of Christianity is easy to join because it rarely asks us to deny ourselves, take up our cross, and follow Him.

A few years ago, I brought a special guest on the air—someone I had just recently met. David Nelms is the founder and president of the Timothy Initiative, a global disciple-making movement working in some of the most hostile regions of the world. Since 2007, they have reached and are discipling nearly 2.5 million people. The cost of discipleship in these places is staggering: loss of family, burned homes, beatings, imprisonment, even death. And yet, in the middle of the pain and discomfort, millions are joyfully following Jesus. David said something when I was interviewing him on the radio that sucked the air out of the room. "Jesus never told us to plant churches," he said. "Jesus told us to make disciples. If you make disciples, they will form strong churches—resilient churches—that can endure

> In places where following Jesus can cost your life, the church is not built on convenience. It is built on conviction.

anything."[2] Church planting is not a bad thing. I'm a church planter in Chicago, but the main thing is disciple-making, and we must keep the main thing the main thing.

In places where following Jesus can cost your life, the church is not built on convenience. It is built on conviction. We crippled discipleship with convenience, but building up those with strong conviction could lead us back to what Jesus actually commanded. Discipleship was never meant to be an optional layer of the Christian life or a ministry track for the especially committed. It *is* the Christian life. Dallas Willard put it plainly:

> The greatest issue facing the world today . . . is whether those who are identified as Christians will become disciples—students, apprentices, practitioners—of Jesus Christ.[3]

Paul's words in Galatians 1:9 could not be clearer: If anyone is preaching to you a gospel contrary to the one you received, let him be accursed. This "different gospel" is one that preserved crowds, protected institutions, and promised life in their own strength. These preachers were not those who walked away, but who stayed and altered the message.

Paul's warning must still be heard. And yet, even here, hope is not extinguished. Consider Martin Luther. Before the Reformation, Luther was not an outsider to a false system—he was one of its most devoted servants. He taught and defended a gospel entangled with fear, penance, and merit. But when Scripture and Spirit finally broke through—when justification by faith alone became clear—Luther repented publicly and risked everything to return to the true gospel. His story stands as proof that even those who once distorted the message can, by grace, be reclaimed.

I'm calling for a spiritual reclamation movement—for leaders and all followers of Jesus willing to admit their subtle addiction to "another gospel," lay it down, and tremble again at the Word of God. Deception does not have to be our destiny. As long as there is breath, clarity remains possible. Jesus said, "Let your light shine before others, so that they may see your good works and give glory to your Father who is in heaven" (Matt. 5:16). Often, truth returns—not through argument, but through lives that finally look like the gospel they proclaim.

FIVE DEADLY ASSUMPTIONS

What cripples disciple-making can be restored. Remembering the call of Jesus Himself: "Go therefore and make disciples of all nations teaching them to observe all that I have commanded you" (Matt. 28:19–20). When the church drifts from that mandate, we inevitably begin measuring the wrong things, rewarding the wrong things, and celebrating the wrong things.

Over the years, I have watched churches of every size wrestle with this. Most pastors know discipleship is their calling. I have seen thriving churches where people were genuinely growing in Christ, and I have seen stagnant churches where spiritual growth was nearly nonexistent. I have seen churches with immense resources deeply committed to disciple-making, and I have seen small churches quietly dying behind the comforting illusion that smaller automatically means healthier.

What I have learned is this: Disciple-making is not usually crippled by bad intentions. It is crippled by deadly assumptions. Assumptions we inherit, those we repeat. Assumptions we rarely challenge because they sound spiritual, practical, or familiar.

Below are five deadly assumptions that I believe are crippling disciple-making in the Western church—and increasingly around the world today.

Deadly Assumption #1: Smaller Is Always Better

There is a growing belief that smaller churches naturally produce deeper disciples. But smaller does not necessarily mean healthier, warmer, or more spiritually vibrant. I led a church in Alaska that grew to be the largest in the state. We had scores of staff, and I watched people flourish spiritually in remarkable ways. There was such a spirit of awakening and hunger for God that stories of transformed lives constantly surfaced. People were growing, serving, repenting, reconciling, and walking closely with Christ.

I have also seen small churches that were spiritually cold, stagnant, and disconnected. Size was never the determining factor. Many people assume that individuals "get lost" in large churches. But the truth is, people can remain just as unknown in a church of fifty as they can in a church of five thousand. The issue is not church size. The issue is whether a culture of intentional disciple-making exists.

Deadly Assumption #2: Disciple-Making Is for a Few Gifted People

Many churches quietly treat disciple-making like a specialized ministry for particularly gifted Christians. But Scripture never presents disciple-making that way. Disciple-making is the collective work of the body of Christ. Every believer is called to participate. Some are gifted in leadership, others in mercy, teaching, encouragement, helps, administration, or hospitality. But all of those gifts are meant to serve the same purpose: helping people grow into maturity in Christ.

There is no spiritual gift called "disciple-making." There are simply believers faithfully using their God-given gifts to help one another follow Jesus. Biblical disciple-making involves helping people access the transforming grace of God—grace that trains us "to renounce ungodliness and worldly passions, and to live self-controlled, upright, and godly lives in the present age" (Titus 2:12). Healthy disciple-making cultures are built when the whole body functions as the body.

Deadly Assumption #3: Small Groups Make Disciples

Small groups can be incredibly helpful. But simply placing people in small groups does not guarantee spiritual growth. Groups can easily become knowledge-broker huddles where people discuss good information every week but never apply truth to their lives. Others become circles of vulnerability where people repeatedly share struggles but receive little meaningful help, support, or biblical direction. Eventually the vulnerability dries up because nobody is changing, growing, and putting sin to death.

Disciple-making is far more than gathering people together. It is helping people become apprentices of Jesus Christ. That requires knowing people well enough to understand where they are struggling, where they are deceived, where they are weak, and what next steps they need to take spiritually. It requires biblical wisdom, relational investment, courage, prayer, truth, encouragement, and practical obedience. Small groups can support disciple-making. But small groups themselves are not by default disciple-making.

Deadly Assumption #4: Discipleship Requires Step-by-Step Curriculum

Many churches love systems, pathways, and predictable processes. And while structure can be helpful, spiritual growth is never mechanical. Every believer grows differently because every believer battles different strongholds, fears, temptations, wounds, distractions, and idols.

One person may need to learn how to put sin to death. Another may need to redeem time and reorder priorities. Someone else may need years of lies dismantled because of deep wounds from childhood. Another may need to separate from destructive friendships that continually pull them away from Christ. Still others are drowning in activity but neglecting intimacy with God. Some possess theological knowledge but have never learned simple obedience.

There are foundational truths every disciple must embrace, but true disciple-making always requires personalized application. Healthy churches create cultures where people are known well enough to receive individualized help as they follow Christ.

Deadly Assumption #5: When You're Born Again You're a Disciple of Jesus

One of the most damaging assumptions in the modern church is that conversion and discipleship are the same thing. They are connected, but they are not identical. The moment a person is born again, they belong to Christ. But that does not mean they are intentionally following Christ or equipped to do it. Scripture repeatedly warns God's kids about being influenced by fools, mockers, scoffers, false teachers, empty philosophies, deceptive traditions, worldly wisdom, sinful desires, and the patterns of the world. Why? Because every person is being discipled by someone or something. Our attention, affections, habits, and beliefs are constantly being shaped, whether intentionally or unintentionally. Everyone follows something and Jesus calls us to follow Him.

Without a deliberate commitment to follow Jesus, believers can find themselves increasingly shaped by culture, politics, entertainment, social media, materialism, self-help ideology, celebrity personalities, and even unbiblical teaching. The New Testament never assumes that spiritual growth happens automatically. It calls believers to abide, follow, learn, obey, and be transformed. Salvation is a free gift received in a moment; discipleship is a lifelong pursuit. Even genuinely born-again people must make discipleship intentional.

WHERE HAVE ALL OUR CHILDREN GONE?

My bride (that's what I call my wife, Junanne, of thirty-nine years) has a list of forty-three adult children of dear friends. These kids were raised in church, most were baptized, and they were all very involved in the life of church throughout their teen years. Their parents, our friends, are imperfect but dynamite moms and dads. They've cried tears, confessed anything they can own that makes their children resent the church, and love them well to this day. But these forty-three kids have left the church and have no interest in aligning their lives with God and His Word. What happened?

You may have heard of people "deconstructing" their faith. I've spoken with at least a dozen people who claim to have done so, and each time it became clear very quickly that they weren't dismantling a life built on the foundation of Jesus Christ—they were walking away from something that never truly existed. They had been culturized into the church but were never truly in Christ.

This is where the truth in 1 John 2:19 comes into sharp focus: "They went out from us, but they were not of us; for if they had been of us, they would have continued with us. But they went out, that it might become plain that they all are not of us." There are certainly exceptions—some people who are genuinely in Christ but become derailed for a season. Yet my conviction is that the vast majority were never truly in Christ, which is why they walked away and now show little evidence of either the life of God within or of the power of the gospel that changes everything.

And if I'm describing your children, do not give up: God is at work and we hear stories of prodigals coming home, and many parents hold on to signs of hope amid the brokenness.

But what collapsed wasn't faith in Christ, but a religious structure, a cultural Christianity that looked solid until the storms came. Their faith looked real but was fake. The counsel I often give to heartsick parents is so counterintuitive: Don't pray first that your children return to church; pray that they are found *in Christ*. Because when they truly come into relationship with their Savior—they recognize His voice and hunger for His presence and, in time, they seek out others who belong to Him as well. Genuine Christ followers have a hunger and thirst for fellowship.

We did not lose a generation because the gospel is weak. We presented it poorly. The epidemic of those leaving the church in the last two decades is not surprising. You can't leave something you were never in.

One verse gives us the framework for understanding much of the exodus we've witnessed from the church: "They went out from us, but they were not of us; for if they had been of us, they would have continued with us. But they went out, that it might become plain that they all are not of us" (1 John 2:19).

> Dead people may attend, agree, admire, sing, and even serve—but they cannot follow Christ.

As heartbreaking as that reality is, it accounts for only part of the problem. It says nothing of the many who remain in our churches, faithfully attending week after week, yet who have never truly belonged to Christ through genuine repentance and faith. That reality may be even more troubling, and it is crippling disciple-making.

There are few things more sobering than finally realizing that something that has long frustrated you has a name—another gospel, which is no gospel at all. Most of us know that nagging sense that there's got to be more. You can't quite articulate it, but you feel it deeply. Things are supposed to be working differently than this. Why does it seem like we make so little progress on the path of following Jesus? What has happened to the children?

When we lower the bar for salvation, we lower the bar for sanctification. We clear the bar but experience little to nothing of the abundant life. We move people into spiritual systems and service opportunities, assuming something that may not be there, measure activity as growth, and call it a success—while something deeper is missing—the soul is left unchanged.

No one is suggesting that disciple-making should be easy. Nothing of eternal value is painless. Jesus promised cost, spiritual battles, perseverance, and suffering. Spiritual growth involves warfare; it requires endurance. But there is a difference between necessary difficulty and self-inflicted dysfunction.

Here is the reality we must face: It is impossible to disciple lost people.

That statement is not cynical; it is biblical. Discipleship assumes a new life, new leader, new direction. It assumes regeneration. It sees the indwelling work of the Holy Spirit. Scripture tells us plainly that apart from Christ we are "dead in (our) trespasses" (Col. 2:13). Dead people do not grow, they do not obey at a soul level, they do not bear fruit. They may attend, agree, admire, sing, give and even serve—but they cannot follow Christ.

It's far easier to gather a crowd than it is to make disciples. Crowds respond to momentum, personality, and programming. Disciple-making, on the other hand, is slow, loving work. It is hard work best done on our knees and with people who exhibit a genuine hunger to follow Jesus. That hunger is precisely what the word *disciple* implies—a learner. An apprentice.

Without it, what we are left with is not discipleship, but image management.

"WHO BEWITCHED YOU?"

I was in San Francisco with a few friends on a warm summer night. We were down at Fisherman's Wharf, where the air buzzed with tourists, street musicians, and entertainers competing for attention. We stopped to watch a guy doing a short presentation built around sleight of hand. He was inviting and genuinely good at what he did.

At one point, he offered someone in the crowd twenty dollars if they could guess where a card would end up after a series of rapid shuffles and dramatic movements. A young woman raised her hand confidently, pulled out her own twenty-dollar bill, and named her choice. She was right. He handed her his twenty, and she kept hers.

I was officially sucked in. The world around me went quiet. I couldn't hear the noise of the Wharf, the music, or the conversations behind me. I was going to beat this game.

The man then invited several more people to step forward—about a dozen of us at once. Each of us handed over our money. I was certain I knew exactly where the card was. Every single one of us was wrong. This man had done this trick hundreds of times and had pocketed thousands of dollars. And I was just another person who thought, *I see it now*, only to realize too late that I had been completely played by the trickster and probably by the young woman working with him.

That is exactly the word the apostle Paul uses in Galatians chapter 3. "O foolish Galatians! Who has bewitched you?" (Gal. 3:1). Paul is not suggesting mild confusion. He is describing enchantment, drawn into something that feels convincing but is fundamentally deceptive and demonic. The Galatians hadn't rejected the gospel outright. They hadn't abandoned Jesus. They had simply been captivated by something that *looked* spiritual but subtly shifted the source of power.

> We have embraced a gospel of *it's up to you*. A gospel of *try harder*.

They had been bewitched by a discipleship model that depended more on the self-striving, self-effort, self-help—what Scripture calls the flesh—than on the very Spirit of God. And that is what makes it so dangerous. It is mesmerizing because human nature insists, *I can do this*. The gospel says, *No, you can't*. And not only that—God never intended for you to.

Scripture invites us to what a close friend of mine calls the throne room of *I will do it for you*. "Let us then with confidence draw near to the throne of grace, that we may receive mercy and find grace to help in time of need" (Heb. 4:16). Grace is not God helping us help ourselves. Grace is God doing for us what we could never do on our own.

That throne room—*I will do it for you*—is the most freeing reality in true discipleship. It is all God. It has always been all God. Jesus made this unmistakably clear: "Apart from me you can do nothing" (John 15:5). Not *a little less*. Not *with diminished results*. Nothing. And yet, in the same breath, Jesus says that it is to the Father's glory that we "bear much fruit." The glory goes to God precisely because the power never came from us.

The problem is that we keep trying to be branches that generate life from within ourselves—mustering enough internal energy to produce something good. And it is impossible. When we fail to cling to Christ, we don't just struggle; we are seduced by an earthbound, impotent approach to discipleship. We are bewitched. And in the process, we have crippled disciple-making.

What we have functionally embraced is a gospel of *it's up to you*. A gospel of *try harder*. One day, it finally clicked for me: Much of what we are doing in the church is turning people into behavior modifiers rather than Jesus abiders. We assume that if people just work a little harder at applying truth, transformation will follow. But we are drowning in image management and totally missing the power of being conformed into the image of Christ.

Jesus addresses this directly in the Sermon on the Mount. Two people hear the same truth. Both face the same storms. Both have the same aspirations. The difference is not knowledge. They both heard the same truth. The difference is not aspiration. They both want a life that is built to last. The difference is obedience empowered by God. One hears and does. The other hears and does nothing. One builds on the rock. The other keeps building on sand—content to know more and more while never applying truth. The former withstands storms, the other falls.

The gospel of knowing more and trying harder is permeating church culture. You may have felt that pressure for years. The gospel of *it's on you* is the voices we hear whispered in our heads. Demonic forces take this twisted gospel and run with it. The gospel of knowledge brokering and self-effort instead of life-changing power is deadly. And it paints an uncomfortably accurate picture of what we are experiencing across churches in the West—and far beyond. But God has so much more.

RECLAIM DISCIPLE-MAKING

This is where disciple-making must be reclaimed, not as a program, but as a way of life. Richard Foster warned that "superficiality is the curse of our age,"[4] and he was right. Formation is slow, intentional, and costly. It requires practices that shape desire, relationships that tell the truth, and communities that aim at applying truth more than acquiring truth. The goal is not more informed Christians, but transformed ones.

Transformation requires intent and action. Jen Wilkin states it beautifully: "We will not wake up ten years from now and find we have passively taken on the character of God."[5] This pursuit of character is not passive; it must be intentional and observable. First to yourself and then to others. The early church changed the world not by lowering the bar, but by lifting high the beauty of Christ and trusting the Spirit to do the work.

The turnaround is possible. We have seen it before, and we are seeing it again—in persecuted regions, quiet living rooms, and faithful communities that refuse to settle for less. The Spirit of God has not grown tired. The mission of Jesus has not changed. What is required is courage—the courage to tell the truth, to measure what actually matters, and to follow Jesus all the way.

The gospel ends where it began: unstoppable. It does not depend on cultural favor, institutional strength, or numerical success. It advances through surrendered lives, faithful disciples, and men and women who take Jesus at His word. This is not a lament for what has been lost. It is a call to reclaim it—for the sake of souls and for the glory of God.

Nine Ways to Know You Stand with God and He Stands with You

Scripture gives unmistakable evidence of genuine faith. In this article you will find nine ways to know you stand with God and He stands with you. My hope is that this serves as a catalyst to confirm that you are truly born again, provide you help if you're not, and inspire you to be a disciple of Christ.

Unstoppablegospel.com/stand

Part Two

CHAMPIONING TRUTH

Chapter 4

THE CURSE

The waves were crashing over the bow of the *Jean M*, a thirty-two-foot fishing vessel I spent several seasons on in Bristol Bay, commercial fishing for sockeye salmon. Anyone who has worked those waters knows they are not forgiving. Weather can turn in minutes. Seas build fast. And when they do, they expose every weakness—of the boat and of the men running it.

CLARITY

On this particular day, the danger wasn't just the waves. Between where we were motoring in Ugashik and where we wanted to set our nets lay miles of other fishermen's gear. Gill nets stretched across the water, often invisible in rough conditions, marked only by cork lines that were nearly impossible to see when visibility dropped.

That matters, because if you roll over another fisherman's gear, it doesn't just inconvenience someone—it can destroy gear and leave boats dead in the water. The lines get sucked into the spinning propeller. Cork lines and then lead lines wrap around the prop shaft in seconds. The engine seizes. You're done. Now you're helpless in heavy seas, drifting without power, and you've mangled another fisherman's net in the process. It's a total mess, and I've experienced it. Boats have been lost that way. Lives too.

The real problem that day was visibility. Sheets of saltwater were slamming over the cabin windows, coating the glass faster than the windshield wipers could clear it. The wipers thrashed back and forth, but they were useless. Salt residue built up in layers, making the windows look like frosted glass. We could hear the waves and feel the roll of the boat. But we could barely see where we were going. And when you can't see, you don't just feel uneasy—you are in real danger.

> When gospel clarity is lost, people drift. But when the gospel is clear, people can see, avoid destruction, and move toward life.

That season, I learned one of the most important lessons of my commercial fishing career. After that day, before every fishing period, I'd take a bottle of Rain-X and thickly coat the cabin windows. I learned quickly that one coat wasn't enough. It needed to be layered up. Then when we set out and those walls of saltwater slammed into the glass, something incredible happened. The water didn't stick. It didn't smear. It didn't cloud the view. It just rolled off. No windshield wipers. No panic. Just clarity.

For hours—sometimes an entire day—we could see clearly where we were going. We could spot cork lines. We could avoid danger. Even when the seas didn't calm down, we could navigate them. It was a total game changer for commercial fishing.

That image captures what happens when gospel clarity is lost—and what happens when it is restored. When the gospel is unclear, people's lives are at risk. They stumble blindly into hazards they cannot see. They get tangled and immobilized, and often become a danger to themselves and to others. But when the gospel is clear—when it coats the windows of the soul and mind—people can see and they can now help others navigate around danger. They can avoid destruction and move toward life.

Scripture says it plainly:

> And even if our gospel is veiled, it is veiled to those who are perishing. In their case the god of this world has blinded the minds of the unbelievers, to keep them from seeing the light of the gospel of the glory of Christ who is the image of God. (2 Cor. 4:3–5)

The crisis facing the church today is not a lack of passion, not even of sincerity or activity. It is a lack of clarity. The god of this age is Satan. He wants to cloud the gospel and he'll use willing accomplices.

CLARIFYING THE CURSE

The gospel is unstoppable when we clearly understand the high stakes. Before it ever sounds like good news, it confronts us with the bad news. Scripture names that bad news with a word we rarely use but desperately need: curse. "For all who rely on works of the law are under a curse; for it is written, 'Cursed be everyone who does not abide by all things written in the Book of the Law, and do them'" (Gal. 3:10). Paul reaches back to the law for a reason: no one keeps it. No one has ever loved God perfectly, obeyed

> This is gospel clarity: seeing the problem clearly enough that the solution finally makes sense.

Him completely, or sustained flawless devotion for a lifetime. The law was never given as a ladder by which we climb our way to God; it stands as a mirror exposing that we cannot. Every human-centered effort to gain or attain a relationship with God collapses under the weight of the curse. Our problem is not performance; it is inherent sinfulness.

The problem is not merely that the world is broken; it is that we are. Left to ourselves, we stand guilty before a holy God.

Not falsely accused—guilty.

Not unlucky—condemned.

Not principally needing liberty from people or earthly systems—but needing liberty from our own sinful selves.

Until we see the reality of the curse, we will never grasp the necessity of the cure. We will shrink the gospel down to environment, therapy, politics, or self-improvement. Clarity begins when we stop blaming what's outward facing and face the inward rebellion of our heart.

But in the same letter that Paul writes with brutal honesty about the curse, he announces an even stronger cure. "Christ redeemed us from the curse of the law by becoming a curse for us" (Gal. 3:13). The cure is not a program. It is not a path of moral effort. It is a Person who stepped into our place. Jesus Christ took upon Himself the full weight of the curse—our guilt, our judgment, our condemnation—and broke its power at the cross.

Only God could pay this price of sacrifice because He is fully loving and just, so He took justice on Himself and became the sacrifice for all. The cure is not behavior modification; it is submission to the One who paid our debt in full. The Spirit of God takes what Christ accomplished and brings it to life in us—awakening us and leading us out of condemnation into freedom. The Spirit moves us from curse to cure, from death to life, from self-effort to Spirit-empowered transformation. That is gospel clarity: seeing the problem clearly enough that the solution finally makes sense.

Consider the apostle Paul. Once a persecutor of the church then radically transformed by the risen Christ, Paul did not deal in vague spiritual language. He told us exactly what the gospel is. Writing to the Corinthians, he said:

> Now I would remind you, brothers, of the gospel I preached to you . . . by which you are being saved. . . . For I delivered to you as of first importance what I also received: that Christ died for our sins in accordance with the Scriptures, that he was buried, that he was raised on the third day in accordance with the Scriptures. (1 Cor. 15:1–4)

This was the good news of an apostle who had been radically transformed by Jesus Christ. If anyone understood the gospel, it was Paul. And he makes it unmistakably clear: Christ died for our sins. Christ was buried. Christ was raised. The curse confronted. The cure accomplished.

As Timothy Keller put it with piercing simplicity, "You are more sinful and flawed than you ever dared believe, and you are more loved and accepted in Jesus Christ than you ever dared hope."[1] That is the gospel—clear enough to expose the curse and powerful enough to deliver the cure. It has been frequently said that God cannot heal who we pretend to be but only who we really are. Humble honesty about ourselves is where clarity begins, and that is where true transformation starts.

THIS OR THAT

The unstoppable gospel calls us to see ourselves through the lens of truth. Demonic forces are desperate to keep us from seeing ourselves as we are. There is no lack of clarity when we face the truth: Scripture reveals either life in Christ or the path of death, and every heart is called to decide between surrender and self, faith and unbelief, repentance and regret. Clarity only exists when "this or that" are unmistakable, and they are. Scripture never presents the gospel as a soft middle ground. It presents stark contrasts. Two responses. Life or death. So let's get clear about the gospel. My appeal to you is bold: Look with clarity for your sake and for those you love. Lives are at risk.

Self-Will vs. Surrender

The crisis of the human soul is not confusion—it is self-rule. From the opening pages of Scripture, sin is portrayed as the refusal to trust God's authority. It is the declaration, *I will decide what is right for me.* That posture does not soften over time; it hardens. In Stephen's speech in Acts 7, he reminded the Israelites of their history. "You stiff-necked people . . . you always resist the Holy Spirit" (v. 51). And we tend toward the same today.

Self-will is stiff-necked pride. It resists the yoke of being partnered, guided, and submitted to God for direction in life. It hears God's Word and says, *Not yet. Not fully. Not on those terms.* The gospel confronts that posture with a call for complete surrender. "If anyone would come after me, let him deny himself and take up his cross daily and follow me" (Luke 9:23). Surrender is not partial obedience; it is the transfer of ownership. "You are not your own, for you were bought with a price" (1 Cor. 6:19–20). Where self-will clings, surrender bows. And only one leads to life.

The Broad Road vs. the Narrow Way

We tend to focus on perception: how others see us walking through life. Jesus challenges us to see not how we're walking but what direction we're heading. "Enter by the narrow gate. For the gate is wide and the way is easy that leads to destruction, and those who enter by it are many. For the gate is narrow and the way is hard that leads to life, and those who find it are few" (Matt. 7:13–14). The broad road demands no repentance, no surrender, no transformation. It accommodates pride and validates self-direction.

The narrow way requires letting go of idols that could never fill our "God-shaped void," a common metaphor for our thirst for God. The narrow way is for those who say no to what was. "Any one of you who does not renounce all that he has cannot be my disciple" (Luke 14:33). The narrow path is entered with empty hands and an open heart. Gospel clarity does not blur these two different paths, but exposes them.

Unbelief vs. Faith

Scripture treats unbelief not as a lack of information, but as a posture of stubborn rebellion. "The light has come into the world, and people loved the darkness rather than the light because their works were evil" (John 3:19). Unbelief withholds trust and allegiance. Faith, by contrast, is not intellectual agreement—it is reliance that trusts God for what we can't see or imagine. "Now faith is the assurance of things hoped for, the conviction of things not seen" (Heb. 11:1).

Saving faith entrusts the whole self to Christ. "Whoever believes in the Son has eternal life; whoever does not obey the Son shall not see life" (John 3:36). What kind of belief saves? Belief that leans into the arms of God even more so than when you lean into a secure railing on the fifty-second floor of a high-rise patio, which can be hair-raising. You have a clear sense that God can hold you, protect you, and keep you from falling. So you throw every square inch of who you are into trusting God.

Regret vs. Repentance

Scripture draws a razor-sharp line between grief that produces life and grief that leaves people dead. "Godly grief produces a repentance that leads to salvation without regret, whereas worldly grief produces death" (2 Cor. 7:10). I like to say there are two kinds of tears that can be cried. One set flows from regret yet the heart remains guarded and alone. The other tears are born of repentance—grief that bows, breaks, and turns toward God.

> Repentance is not an accessory to faith; it is the doorway into it.

The New Testament word for repentance is *metanoia*, which means a change of mind—not broadened thinking, but a radical transformation of one's inner disposition, a turning around or conversion that reorients the way a person thinks, feels, and wills, resulting in a decisive change in life direction. Regret feels deeply while stubbornly holding on to self; repentance feels deeply and surrenders self to God.

That distinction matters because the gospel Jesus preached—and sent His disciples out to proclaim—was first and foremost a gospel of repentance. The opening declaration of His ministry is unmistakable: "The time is fulfilled, and the kingdom of God is at hand; repent and believe in the gospel" (Mark 1:15).

Repentance is not an accessory to faith; it is the doorway into it. We were all born with our backs to God so the door is behind us, and we can't walk through it without turning. Grace does not alleviate the need for repentance; it produces it. And the true opposite of repentance is not ignorance or apathy, but resistance—a settled refusal to yield to God's rightful rule. Where resistance remains, there may be emotion, even tears, but no transformation. Where *metanoia* occurs, resistance collapses, the will bends, and life truly begins.

Death vs. Life

God framed the human condition in stark, uncompromising terms when He spoke through Moses: "I have set before you life and death, blessing and curse" (Deut. 30:19). That is not theory—it is covenant prophecy. Scripture insists we are not born spiritually neutral or merely underperforming; we are born under the curse, separated from God, "dead in the trespasses and sins" (Eph. 2:1). Death is our native condition. Which means salvation is not God improving an otherwise living person, not Jesus helping us become a better version of ourselves—it is God intervening where there is no life at all. The gospel does not decorate the corpse; it raises the dead.

This is why the New Testament speaks of salvation in resurrection language.

"But God . . . made us alive together with Christ" (Eph. 2:4–5).

"If anyone is in Christ, he is a new creation" (2 Cor. 5:17).

A reborn person "has passed from death to life" (John 5:24).

Jesus Himself said your life cannot be tweaked or supplemented—you must be born again (John 3:3). This is not a subtle shift, not a moral upgrade, not a religious add-on; it is a decisive transfer from one realm to another. Death to life. Curse to blessing. Old creation to new. Miss that, and everything else becomes cosmetic. See it, and you finally understand why the gospel is not modification of behavior—it is resurrection of the dead.

False Assurance vs. Saving Faith

False assurance settles for the appearance of faith without the reality of transformation. It rests on memories, powerful moments, prayers once prayed, or correct behavior performed, while the heart remains fundamentally unchanged. It confuses exposure to truth with submission to truth, proximity to Jesus with participation in His life. Jesus warned that many would say the right words, "Lord, Lord," and still be unknown to Him (Matt. 7:21–23). False assurance is content with belief that does not bend the will, dethrone sin, or produce perseverance. It offers confidence without repentance, hope without surrender, and peace without reconciliation—and in doing so, it inoculates the soul against the very gospel that could save it.

Saving faith, by contrast, is not merely believing something about Jesus but entrusting oneself to Him. It is faith that unites the sinner to Christ, producing repentance, obedience, and endurance—not as add-ons, but as evidence of life. Scripture describes it as a faith that works through love. This faith bears fruit, and holds fast to the end (see Gal. 5:6; John 15:8; Heb. 3:14). Saving faith does not boast in decision or sincerity, but in Christ alone. False assurance asks, "Am I safe?" Saving faith asks, "Am I His?"

God does not blur the path before us; He clarifies it. From beginning to end, Scripture presents not a foggy spectrum of options but a clear, merciful contrast—this or that, life or death, narrow path or broad road, repentance or regret. The Lord paints a merciful picture of two paths. One leads to life. The other leads to death.

That kind of clarity is not harsh—it is love. Love speaks plainly. Love tells the truth. Love refuses to let us drift toward destruction without warning. In a world addicted to ambiguity, God's clarity is mercy. This is what makes the gospel unstoppable. It tells the truth about where each decision leads and invites every person to step into life. It is what every person on the planet deserves to hear, what every wandering son or daughter needs to see, and what every cultural Christian must be lovingly confronted with—for the sake of their lives now and for eternity.

A CALL TO THOSE WHO LOVE

When we compare Jesus' clear words with the often foggy and diluted message of cultural Christianity, it becomes painfully evident why discipleship has grown so shallow.

Week after week, good, Bible-believing churches, both in the West and even globally, are filled with people who assume they are in Christ but have never truly encountered the transforming power of the gospel. With the absence of gospel clarity and the inexpressible beauty of *sola fide*, faith alone, two challenges result:

1. Painstaking attempts to make disciples of lost people, an impossibility.

2. Growth bends toward human effort because we lose the wonder of Christ's power alone to save us from the curse and change those He saves.

But this is not a moment for despair—it is a moment for hope. The unstoppable gospel is not vague. It is vibrantly clear. It cuts through confusion, exposes what is false, and calls people into what is real. Every person deserves a fair hearing of what the gospel truly is: life-giving truth that moves us from death to life. Clarity can hurt because truth cuts deeply. But clarity is mercy. Clarity is love. And when the gospel is seen and heard as it truly is, it can do what God always intended: transform lives and make disciples.

Our task is not to soften the message or lower the bar to get more people over, but to clear the window.

For anyone who leads and anyone who loves—a pastor, preacher, small-group leader, parent, grandparent, Sunday school teacher, friend, neighbor—this is the call before us: gospel clarity. In Bristol Bay, danger wasn't the sea—it was what you couldn't see. A few passes with Rain-X didn't change the weather or calm the water, but it cleared the glass. Suddenly the horizon came into view.

That's our calling. We are not asked to manufacture results; we are entrusted with the message of reconciliation as ambassadors for Christ (2 Cor. 5:17–20). Our task is not to soften the message or lower the bar to get more people over, but to clear the window—so Christ, repentance, faith, and life can be seen plainly. Even when there is a public call to respond, as on the day of Pentecost, the power was never in the results of the moment itself but in the clarity of what was proclaimed.

This is how Jesus taught. He cleared the fog with pictures and contrasts—blindness and sight—so people could see what was real. "The people dwelling in darkness have seen a great light" (Matt. 4:16). Clarity doesn't remove danger, but it can keep people from ending up tangled and dead in the water because they never saw what was coming. And when the gospel window is clean—and Christ is proclaimed as Lord, repentance is named, faith is called for, and life is offered—the Spirit of God does what only He can do: opens blind eyes, raises the dead, brings people from darkness into light.

That's gospel clarity. And like a cleared windshield in high seas, it can mean the difference between destruction and life.

The Most Terrifying Words Jesus Ever Spoke

Many will stand before Jesus on the day of judgment, fully convinced they belong to Him, only to be shocked that He will say "depart from me." Watch this discussion I have with Dr. Erwin Lutzer on Matthew 7 and understand why such a vast number of people will be tragically wrong.

Unstoppablegospel.com/depart

Chapter 5

THE CURE

If someone could just cast some demons out of me, I was sure my life would change. That was my diagnosis.

By my early twenties, my life was unraveling. Cocaine had become a raging addiction and alcohol was my nightly landing gear—just enough to bring me down so I could wake up and do it all over again. The parties were fulfilling at some level, but the emptiness afterward was overwhelming.

THE DEVIL MADE ME DO IT

I had been thoroughly culturized in Christianity. I had walked aisles, prayed prayers, been baptized, and absorbed enough biblical knowledge to believe I stood with God and God stood with me. I knew the jargon, and just enough about demons and spiritual warfare to believe there was an explanation for why my life remained so out of control. "If demons were the issue, then demons could be cast out," I thought. Someone with enough spiritual authority could do for me what I apparently could not do for myself.

I had cried out to God more than once, promising that if He would rescue me, I would finally get serious about Him. One of those prayers came after a package of cocaine was seized by federal agents at Anchorage International Airport with my name on it. It was a terrifying few days. In the chaos of my fear, I offered God the kind of desperate foxhole prayer many people pray when they are cornered: "Lord, if You get me out of this, I promise I'll get my life together."

The crisis passed, but my heart did not change. Before long, I found myself right back in the same destructive cycle. That was when I called Keith, who'd been my pastor in childhood, and asked if he would meet with me. I told him I had some roadblocks in my life and needed his help removing them.

Keith was no stranger to this territory. Growing up, I had heard story after story about him helping people in genuine spiritual bondage. Some of those accounts were hair-raising, but they all reinforced the same conclusion in my mind: Keith knew how to help people get free. When he arrived at my home, I was bracing for something dramatic. After some small talk, he began asking me questions about Jesus Christ—who He was, what I believed about Him, and whether I understood the gospel.

As he looked piercingly into my eyes, I wondered what might happen next. Would I lose control of my body? Would I fall off the couch and twitch on the floor? Would something dark and terrifying manifest itself out of my mouth? None of that happened. After nearly two hours, Keith stood up, leaned toward me, and said words that landed like a gut punch. "Karl, you don't have a demon problem. You have a Karl problem." And he walked out. It was awkward and I felt hopeless.

It would be another year before God brought me to the end of myself. I was driving down the frozen streets of Anchorage, Alaska, when a question rose in my heart with unmistakable clarity: "Are you done yet?"

In that moment, the scales fell from my eyes. I realized that I was not merely trapped by destructive habits or oppressed by demonic forces. I was the problem. I had my back to God. I was not just missing the mark; I was in active rebellion against the One who made me. I was both enslaved by sin and fully responsible for it.

That was the day everything changed. Not because a demon was cast out, but because God stripped away my excuses and showed me the truth. What I needed was not deliverance from a satanic force. I needed deliverance from myself. I needed a new heart. I needed Jesus Christ. He was the cure. The gospel did not merely clean up a broken life. It transformed a dead one.

BLESSED ARE THE HONEST

Jesus opens the Sermon on the Mount by exposing our true spiritual condition and promising blessing to those honest enough to see it. "Blessed are the poor in spirit, for theirs is the kingdom of heaven" (Matt. 5:3). Seeing our spiritual poverty for the mess it is takes us to another world. Honesty about our soul's bankrupt condition frees us to experience the riches of another kingdom. Jesus is not praising weakness; He is celebrating and rewarding honesty.

To be poor in spirit is to finally see the truth about ourselves—that apart from God we have nothing. In other words, blessed

> The problem is not merely that our heart is twisted—it is that we can't understand just how twisted it is.

are those who stop pretending they have a little something without God when they don't. Blessed are those who live not by lies and admit their spiritual bankruptcy. Blessed are those who are honest to God. There is no freedom, no healing, no entrance into the kingdom apart from seeing ourselves rightly. Until we acknowledge our poverty, grace feels optional. Once we do, grace becomes indispensable.

Scripture is clear on this point. We are warned repeatedly about our capacity for self-deception. "The heart is deceitful above all things, and desperately sick; who can understand it?" (Jer. 17:9). The problem is not merely that our heart is twisted—it is that we can't understand just how twisted it is. Paul presses hard: "If anyone thinks he is something, when he is nothing, he deceives himself" (Gal. 6:3). God does not flatter us; He tells us the truth so that we might finally stop hiding from it.

This is why the great theologians of the church consistently viewed honest self-knowledge as the doorway of salvation. John Calvin opens *Institutes of the Christian Religion* with these words: "Nearly all the wisdom we possess, that is to say, true and sound wisdom, consists of two parts: the knowledge of God and of ourselves."[1] Calvin understood what we resist—that inflated self-perception clouds our vision of God, and clear sight of God inevitably exposes the truth about us. The gateway to salvation is not self-improvement, but self-exposure—bringing the real us into the light of a holy and perfect God who still loves us.

That is why Jesus' words—"he who has been forgiven little, loves little"—are so often misunderstood (Luke 7:47). This statement has nothing to do with the degree of sin and everything to do with the depth of awareness of just how ugly and destructive our sin really is. And yes, we have all sinned and fall far short of giving God glory. Jesus is not teaching a sliding forgiveness scale where scandalous sinners love Him more than respectable ones. Simon, the Pharisee, was mocking a woman known as a "sinner," that "this sort of woman" (v. 39) would pour out her tears and expensive perfume on Jesus, all the while glossing over his own twisted darkened heart and life. Ignoring the reality that all are "sinners" and all are pitiable.

Jesus is exposing that the deeper our awareness of our need for God produces an overflow of humble gratitude. Simon had not sinned less—he simply saw less sin in himself. He made the classic mistake of judging ourselves by our intentions and others by their actions. Simon did not recognize that, like everyone else, he was born with his back to God (Rom. 3:10–12), and "by nature" he was "a child of wrath" (Eph. 2:1–3). Paul describes this self-deceived condition with sobering clarity: "Their end is destruction, their god is their belly, and they glory in their shame, with minds set on earthly things" (Phil. 3:19). The core issue is not how bad we are—but whether we have ever seen just how twisted, dark, separate, alone, and lost we truly are from birth. This may be difficult to hear, but Scripture paints a picture that the greatest deception is self-righteousness. Thinking we have our lives put together can blind us to our need for God.

That moment of seeing ourselves rightly is both crushing and positions us to be radically changed spiritually. The day God pulled me out of the darkness is almost a blur now. What I remember most clearly is not a list of sins, but a single question that seemed to cut straight through every defense: "Are you done yet?" In that

Until we see ourselves so honestly that our soul is gasping for air, grace remains distant and theoretical.

moment, I was confronted with the reality of who I really was. No longer could the cocaine, the alcohol, the carousing—no longer could any of it mask the truth. It wasn't that I was forgiven *more* because my sins were somehow worse than someone else's. It was that God, in His grace, allowed me to finally see myself for who I was. And what I saw was the same condition Scripture says is true of every one of us apart from Christ—walking dead.

That is the power of the gospel. Not moral reform or religious performance, but the miracle of clear sight. Until we see ourselves so honestly that our soul is gasping for air, grace remains distant and theoretical. But when God, in His mercy, strips away illusion and allows us to see ourselves as we really are before a holy and perfect God, everything changes. That kind of honesty does not lead to despair—it leads to freedom. It is the beginning of genuine spiritual prosperity. Not in pretending we are rich, but in admitting we are poor—and discovering that the kingdom of heaven belongs to people like that.

GOOD GROUND

I had no idea what I was doing. I was just a kid in Anchorage, Alaska, and all I wanted was a small patch of ground to grow something. This region of Alaska is famous for absurdly large vegetables—cabbages the size of beach balls, zucchinis that look like they come from another planet—and I'd heard potatoes would be a good crop to grow. So I asked my dad if I could take over a strip of earth near the house and try my hand at farming. He said yes.

I planted about ten rows. I didn't know much, but I knew enough to work the soil—to turn it over, break it up, and mound it high. I then carefully placed small chunks of potato into the heaped rows. I covered, watered, and walked away. But nothing happened. Not right away.

Days went by. Then more days. I'd come home from running my paper route, playing with friends, or fishing in a nearby lake, and I'd walk straight over to my little "farm," and just stare at the dirt. No green. No movement. No sign that anything was happening at all.

Then one day—without warning—tiny green shoots broke through the soil. Potato plants. Real leaves. Real growth. And once they came, they came fast. Those plants shot up as if they had been waiting their whole lives for permission.

All summer long, under those endless Alaskan daylight hours, the plants exploded. But the real miracle wasn't what I could see. Everything that mattered was happening underground.

When it finally came time to harvest, I put a shovel into the soil, gently lifted it up, and couldn't believe what I found. Potatoes everywhere. We had potatoes for our family, potatoes for neighbors, potatoes for friends. I started handing out bags of potatoes along my paper route. All of that from those little chunks buried deep months earlier.

The miracle wasn't the potato seed. It wasn't sunlight. And it wasn't the watering schedule since I was hopelessly inconsistent. The miracle was in the quality of the soil. And that patch of ground had some rich soil.

That is exactly what Jesus is teaching in the parable of the four soils. Jesus tells us plainly that the seed is good news for sinners, the cure for a world under a curse of sin, and that the soils are the different conditions of the human heart. The message is the

> The word never penetrates. It remains on the surface—hard soil, hard heart.

same—the gospel; the difference is never the message, but where the message lands, that is, the condition of the heart. And Jesus is unmistakably clear: Of the four soils, only one represents a heart that truly receives the word and produces genuine, enduring life. Only one heart condition is ready to receive the newness of life and reproduce it.

Jesus begins with the hard soil: "When anyone hears the word of the kingdom and does not understand it, the evil one comes and snatches away what has been sown in his heart" (Matt. 13:19). The heart condition here is clear: hard hearts are impenetrable even with the clearest truth. It remains on the surface—hard soil, hard heart. There is exposure to truth, but there is no reception, no repentance, no transformation. Nothing takes root. The seed is present for a moment, but it doesn't enter the soil of the heart. And Satan grabs it away.

Then Jesus describes the rocky soil:

> "As for what was sown on rocky ground, this is the one who hears the word and immediately receives it with joy, yet he has no root in himself, but endures for a while, and when tribulation or persecution arises on account of the word, immediately he falls away." (Matt. 13:20–21)

There is real emotion here, enthusiasm. An immediate response that can look remarkably convincing, like they really got it. But there is no depth. No root. No internal transformation that can withstand pressure. When the gospel begins to cost something—like comfort, reputation, or sacrifice—the response collapses. The problem is not persecution. The problem here again is the absence of deep reception. What appeared to be alive is revealed to still be dead.

Then Jesus turns to the thorny soil, perhaps the most culturally familiar of all:

> "As for what was sown among thorns, this is the one who hears the word, but the cares of the world and the deceitfulness of riches choke the word, and it proves unfruitful." (Matt.13:22)

Notice carefully what Jesus says—and what He does not say. The word is heard. There is real exposure. There may even be early signs of growth. Christ is not opposed, but is simply given no space, left to coexist with rival loves that are never dethroned. Over time the word is choked—not by scandalous rebellion alone, but by ordinary life: worry, money, ambition, the pull of other desires. And Jesus' verdict is unmistakable: "It proves unfruitful."

Alistair Begg captures this distinction with striking clarity: "The problem is not that there is open rejection of Christ, but that there is no room for Him."[2] In the thorny soil, Christ may be welcomed, but He is never enthroned; He's present, but not preeminent. He is added to a life still ruled by competing loves. And where Christ is not allowed to rule, the word does not ultimately bear fruit.

This is where we must speak with clarity in our cultural moment. Yes, genuine believers can struggle. Yes, true Christ followers can be entangled or hindered in fruitfulness. Scripture is honest about that. But Jesus is pressing us to consider something deeper: How many lives that appear spiritually responsive have never truly surrendered the throne? How many have allowed Jesus to remain alongside worry, wealth, and the desire for other things without ever allowing Him to reign? The issue is not whether Christ was acknowledged, but whether He was allowed to rule. Where He does not rule, there is no enduring fruit. And where there is no enduring fruit, Jesus does not point to a delayed harvest—He declares an unfruitful soil, an unregenerated soul, a religiously active lost person.

Finally, Jesus describes the good soil: "As for what was sown on good soil, this is the one who hears the word and understands it. He indeed bears fruit and yields, in one case a hundredfold, in another sixty, and in another thirty" (Matt. 13:23). Luke records an additional phrase that sharpens the picture even further: "They are those who, hearing the word, hold it fast in an honest and good heart, and bear fruit with patience" (Luke 8:15).

This soil is not perfect soil. It is receptive soil. The defining mark is not emotional intensity, speed of response, or uniform productivity. It is endurance. The word is held fast. It is received deeply enough to take root and remain. And because there is life, there is fruit. Not identical fruit in every life. Not the same measure or pace. But real fruit—visible evidence of an internal transformation that endures over time.

This is why Jesus allows for thirtyfold, sixtyfold, and hundredfold. The amount varies. His presence does not. Where the word has truly taken root, fruit will follow. J. C. Ryle described the fruit of good soil with pastoral precision: "But effects there always will be; some fruit will always be seen where there is true conversion. Where no effect can be seen, there you may be sure there is no grace. Where no visible fruit can be found, there you may be sure there is no conversion."[3]

Potatoes don't grow on the surface. They grow in deep, good soil. And authentic faith is not a surface play either. Real faith is born and grows in a heart that is honest to God about the need for Him, not to cohabitate with other gods, but singularly rule from the preeminent place of authority. The seed was never the problem. The Sower was never the problem. The soil tells the whole story.

WHO ARE YOU?

It's funny how easily we claim identities that reality doesn't exactly confirm. Someone claims to be a runner, but hasn't laced up shoes in four months. Another insists she's a reader, though she can't remember the last book she read. A person declares he's a great cook, yet his smoke alarm gets more action than his oven. None of this is malicious—it's just human nature. We all recognize the gap. We tend to define ourselves by intention rather than by what our lives consistently produce. And that's where the irony lives: We can say who we are all day long, but eventually reality tells the truth.

And that brings us to another "honest to God" moment that helps us locate where we truly are with God—not emotionally, not culturally, not traditionally, but biblically. It's the difference between a label that can be cheap and a word that cannot.

Take the word "Christian." It literally means "those associated with Christ." In the New Testament, the term appears only three times, a word invented by a mocking world: "In Antioch the disciples were first called Christians" (Acts 11:26); "In a short time would you persuade me to be a Christian?" (Acts 26:28); and "Yet if anyone suffers as a Christian, let him not be ashamed, but let him glorify God in that name" (1 Peter 4:16).

In the first century, "Christian" was not a benign category on a census form. It was a public identifier that would attach

> The word disciple or follower is used about 269 times in the New Testament.

you to a despised, controversial, crucified Messiah—and that identification could cost you reputation, relationships, livelihood, and sometimes your life. In Acts, believers are scattered under persecution (Acts 8:1–3). In Hebrews, they are described as those who "joyfully accepted the plundering of [their] property" because they knew they had a better possession (Heb. 10:34). Peter tells them not to be ashamed if they suffer "as a Christian" (1 Peter 4:16). In other words, in the New Testament world, the label was not a shrug. It was a target.

Now compare that with what "Christian" has become in much of our modern world—often a catchall for someone who is not Muslim, Hindu, atheist, hostile, whatever. In many places, "Christian" can mean "I'm basically a decent person," or "I go to church sometimes," or "I believe in God," or "I was raised this way." It can be a cultural inheritance rather than a crucified identity. And that gap—between New Testament cost and modern convenience—should make us pause long enough to be honest to God.

But the dominant word—the word that towers over the landscape of the Gospels and Acts—is "disciple." The word disciple or follower is used, give or take, 269 times in the New Testament. A true "disciple" is the primary category the New Testament uses to describe the people of Jesus who had an authentic relationship with Him and were willing to pay the price for claiming so.

And a disciple is not merely a church attender or someone who likes Christian ideas. A disciple is a learner, yes, but not in the academic sense. A disciple is a follower, an apprentice. Someone who is being re-formed by their Master. Jesus defined it in costly, concrete terms: "If anyone would come after me, let him deny himself and take up his cross daily and follow me" (Luke 9:23). He spoke of allegiance that outruns earthly ties and that counts the cost before you claim His name (Luke 14:26, 28). He spoke of a kind of proximity: "If you abide in my word, you are truly my disciples" (John 8:31).

A disciple is someone who is no longer negotiating whether Jesus gets to be Lord. The negotiation is over. The followership is real.

THE "Y" IN THE ROAD

So here's the question—and it is meant to be answered in the presence of God, not in the audience of others—Who are you? In our culture, "Christian" can be a convenient label. "Believer" can be reduced to mere assent. But "disciple" is a word with teeth. It describes intent. Direction. Allegiance. It describes someone who has been gripped by Christ and is now being shaped by Him.

And let me say it plainly, because some of the most sincere people I know are the most easily shaken; you may be a stumbling, bumbling disciple. You may be the person who wakes up, puts your feet on the floor, and within an hour you've said something you regret, thought something you're ashamed of, chased something too small, feared something too big. You may feel the thorns choking your affection for Jesus and trying to crowd out what matters most.

But the hallmark of the good soil is not perfection—it is persevering attachment. It is intent on a new direction. It is a heart that truly wants to honor God in the deepest recesses, and when it doesn't, it is grieved, convicted, and brought back by the Spirit of God. That is not performance. That is life, a wrestling with self and Satan to be controlled by Christ alone because He has so radically changed your heart.

Being honest to God means we stop hiding behind a label and we ask the questions the New Testament actually invites us to consider: Is Christ merely present in my life, or is He preeminent? Is the Word being choked, or is it yearning for more? Is there fruit—not flawless or impressive, but real fruit that comes from Christ's life?

One of the clearest descriptors of genuine faith is what Paul celebrates in the church of Thessalonica. He doesn't begin with their programs or knowledge or outward discipline. He points to something far more fundamental—a decisive turn. Look at the report Paul received about their genuine faith:

> For they themselves report concerning us the kind of reception we had among you, and how you turned to God from idols to serve the living and true God, and to wait for his Son from heaven, whom he raised from the dead, Jesus who delivers us from the wrath to come. (1 Thess. 1:9–10)

They turned, laid down idols, and aimed to serve and walk with the living God.

There comes a moment when every person must face this reality: You cannot turn to God with your hands full of the gods of this age. Something must be released. Something has to be abandoned. Idols don't always look like statues; in the West they more often look like self-reliance, control, money, success, approval, comfort, and the quiet belief that we can manage our own lives. But the movement of genuine faith is unmistakable. We turn from dead things to the living God. We turn from what cannot save to the One who alone can. We turn from what we thought would give us life to the One who is life.

Paul's language is stark because the contrast is stark. The curse is death. Every idol, every substitute god, every self-powered attempt at life apart from God eventually leads there. But the cure is Christ. He alone rescues. He alone gives life. He alone sustains what He begins. And when that turning happens—when we release the false gods and cling to the Living One—everything changes. We begin to live in the freedom and expectancy Paul describes: serving the living and true God and waiting for His Son from heaven. That is the rhythm of the with-God life: turning, serving, and trusting—not in ourselves, but in the One who saves and the One who will surely bring us all the way home.

180

And if today is your day of salvation—or if today is the day you stop striving or are awakened to the truth and start dealing honestly with God—then don't complicate what Scripture keeps clear: Repent and believe. Repentance is not the same thing as regret. Regret is feeling bad about consequences. Repentance is a turning; a 180-degree turn, a decisive break with self-rule and sin. It is coming into agreement with God about your sin, not excusing it, not renaming it, not managing it, but confessing it and forsaking it.

Repentance is not cleaning yourself up so God will accept you; it is coming to God because you finally admit you cannot clean yourself up or get yourself together.

Faith is not a vague optimism nor just "I believe in God." Faith is personal trust in the crucified and risen Christ; it's resting the weight of your soul on Him. It is receiving Jesus not merely as a name I claim, but who is yet to be Savior and Lord: ruler, master, and friend. It is leaning on His finished work, not presenting your own. It is taking Him at His word, clinging to Him when you feel unworthy, and obeying Him because you now belong to Him—you are now *with* God and living the with-God life.

And the joy on the other side of that honesty is not anxiety, it's relationship. Not performance, but peace. Not pretending, but assurance grounded in Christ Himself. Because when the soil is made new, the seed goes deep. And in time, by grace, there will be fruit.

Six Ways God Saves Those You Love

The ultimate cure for anyone is a relationship with Jesus Christ—only God can truly change everything. But how does God save those you love? Read this article for six surprising ways He reaches into a person's soul with the cure they desperately need. God is able to save, and He may use you—or someone close to the one you love—to help lead them to Jesus.

Unstoppablegospel.com/cure

Chapter 6

THE WITH-GOD LIFE

Blaise—as in Blaise Pascal—came home with me from Alaska as a young husky pup, tucked under the seat in front of me on a long flight to Chicago. In a matter of hours everything familiar disappeared. The smells, the sounds, his littermates, all gone, replaced by a city pulsing with lots of people, new noises, and two house cats for roommates.

He was learning a whole new world—unsure, a bit cautious, but wide-eyed with curiosity. Every walk felt like discovery. His sniffer worked overtime, tracing every scent. He'd stop mid-stride to watch his first airplanes cut across the sky. His ears would twitch at the distant rumble of trains. Any person he spotted, even from a distance, was a potential friend. The world was new, and he wanted all of it.

We rounded a quiet corner one afternoon with a few birds chirping somewhere in the distance. The leash was tight as he moved ahead of me, exploring but tethered, still with me. Then—wham! A violent eruption of barking shattered the calm. I looked up just in time to see a massive Rottweiler body-slamming a bay window, throwing its full weight against the glass while a smaller dog inside the house joined the frenzy. Both were doing everything they could to crash through that window and get to Blaise. He knew it instantly. He didn't bolt forward or panic and pull away. He slid back—straight to me. Circling and then tight against my legs, so that I stood squarely between him and those brute dogs. He pressed to the far side of my body, silent but certain. So young, yet completely confident I had him covered.

Blaise was modeling a spiritual principle. Because that is the with-God way.

ALL THINGS NEW

The with-God life is a journey into a kingdom where everything becomes new. New sights. New sounds. New challenges and opportunities. Our former life was nothing compared to the with-God life. In the with-God life, blues are bluer, greens are greener, and the sky seems wider. Life with God is not intended to be dull, restrained, or diminished. It is vivid. Awake. Charged with purpose and presence.

As God designed it, there are stretches on this journey when we move out with holy curiosity, exploring what God has made, discovering what it means to walk with Him in real time. And then there are moments when we draw in close, when the leash goes slack and we settle right beside our Savior because we know exactly where our covering is found. We don't panic. We don't posture. We move near.

There's a difference between living *for* God and living *with* God. Living for God keeps Him at a distance and turns life into performance. God's at home and we're out on our own. Living with God keeps Him near and turns life into a dynamic relationship. We walk, run, stumble, and fall but He's right there to pick us up and give us the direction and protection we need.

Most of us have been taught that we live *for* God, and we do. But not independent of God's care and conversation. Spiritual dependence must always precede personal diligence. Few of us have learned to live *with* God. And that may be the greatest loss in modern Christianity. Because somewhere along the way, especially in the Western church, we drifted from a vibrant, dependent, with-God life into something far more self-directed. We talk about God. We work for God. We try to please God. But we often live as though the day-to-day responsibility for growth, strength, and transformation rests squarely on our shoulders. That shift is subtle, but massive. And it has created a quiet exhaustion in the people of God. Parched souls and wandering hearts often result. We're wandering the streets alone. Underfed, unfulfilled, and wondering why faith seems shallow and sometimes empty.

FUNCTIONAL ATHEISM

Here's a word that captures what has quietly happened in much of Western Christianity: *bifurcation.* Bifurcation is simply a division into two separate parts, a separation that was never meant to exist. And that is precisely what has happened in the spiritual lives of countless disciples of Christ. We have allowed a great chasm to form between what we profess and how we function.

We confess Jesus Christ as Lord and Savior, sing of His power, affirm His sovereignty, and then live as though it is largely up to us to make life work. We function as though we are the source of our own growth, strength, and fruit.

This lack of integration has produced what can only be called functional atheism. Not theoretical or ideological. Functional. We believe in God, but we live as though everything ultimately depends on us. We affirm grace but operate by grit.

The result is a bifurcated life—one part devoted to God in belief, the other devoted to self in practice and execution. And that split leaves us spiritually strained and quietly exhausted.

Paul confronted this very tendency in the Galatian believers. Having begun by grace, they were already drifting into self-effort. His words are sharp because the danger is real. "Are you so foolish? Having begun by the Spirit, are you now being perfected by the flesh?" (Gal. 3:3). In other words, did you really think God would raise you from spiritual death only to leave you responsible for sustaining the life He gave you?

We trust Christ for salvation but rely on ourselves for formation. We look to Him for rescue but to ourselves for growth.

The fruit of the Spirit is not the product of human effort, manufactured through willpower or sustained through visible discipline alone. More spiritual activity can't fill the hole in a soul that lacks proximity to God. It is called fruit precisely because it grows from a living source. Love, joy, peace, patience, kindness, goodness, faithfulness, gentleness, self-control—these are not achievements of the self. They are the outgrowth of the Spirit's presence and power within a yielded life. When we attempt to produce them apart from deep dependence on God, we create strain rather than fruit.

> The with-God life draws us back to a moment-by-moment reliance on the Spirit of God to do in us what we could never do on our own.

This bifurcation is deeply embedded in Western thinking. We have been shaped by a mindset that tells us what we can do, we must do. We can even have a "quiet time" with God and toggle into a sense the rest is "my time," hoping the fumes of quietness with God can sustain us. Independence is celebrated, self-sufficiency admired, control assumed. And without realizing it, we import those assumptions directly into our spiritual lives. We trust Christ for salvation but rely on ourselves for formation. We look to Him for rescue but to ourselves for growth. And the result is a divided existence—devoted to God in song and confession, yet devoted to self in the actual mechanics of living.

A. W. Tozer saw this many years ago, "The self-sins are the most deeply rooted and troublesome of all sins. They dwell too deep within us and are too much a part of our natures to come to our attention till the light of God is focused upon them."[1] He understood that self-reliance, even when dressed in religious language, quietly resists the life of dependence God intends.

When this bifurcation takes hold, it renders us spiritually impotent. Not inactive—often we are very busy—but powerless in the deepest sense. We can generate motion, but not transformation. We may maintain appearances, but lack the quiet power that flows from a life truly lived with God.

A fully integrated life looks different. It is a life in which what we confess and how we function are no longer separated. A life in which dependence on God is not reserved for Sunday worship or moments of crises but becomes the steady posture of everyday living. A life in which we stop trying to produce what only God can grow.

The with-God life refuses to live two lives. It refuses the illusion that we can manage our own spiritual formation. Instead, it draws us back to the only place where life truly flourishes, a moment-by-moment reliance on the Spirit of God to do in us what we could never do on our own.

SWEEPING GRACE

Few hymns in the history of the church are as universally known as John Newton's "Amazing Grace."[2] It has been sung across centuries and continents, in cathedrals and country churches, in moments of revival, at secular gatherings, and at bedsides of grief. It is perhaps the most recognized testimony to the power of redeeming grace ever written other than the Bible.

We know it so well that we can almost sing the first verse without thinking. It captures the wonder of a soul found, rescued, awakened, and brought near by mercy we did not deserve and could never earn:

Amazing grace! how sweet the sound
That saved a wretch like me!
I once was lost, but now am found;
Was blind, but now I see.

Those words endure because they capture the miracle of conversion—the moment grace finds us. The moment our eyes are opened. The moment we are brought from death to life, from lost to found, from blindness to sight.

But while that first verse celebrates the radical nature of salvation, the less familiar verses unfold something even more sweeping. Grace not only finds us and saves us; it forms us. The rest of the song reveals that the Christian life was never meant to be lived merely for God, but with Him—sustained moment by moment by the grace that first awakened us.

These next verses reveal the breathtaking scope of grace across the whole of the Christian life:

'Twas grace that taught my heart to fear,
And grace my fears relieved;
How precious did that grace appear
The hour I first believed.

Through many dangers, toils, and snares
I have already come;
'Tis grace hath brought me safe thus far,
And grace will lead me home.

The Lord has promised good to me,
His Word my hope secures;
He will my shield and portion be
As long as life endures.

When we've been there ten thousand years,
Bright shining as the sun;
We've no less days to sing God's praise
Than when we first begun.

Newton grasped a powerful truth we often overlook: Grace is not in play merely at the moment of rescue. It is the fuel of the entire journey. Grace teaches. Relieves. Leads. Secures. Shields. Grace finishes what grace began. From first awakening to final glory, the Christian life unfolds as a with-God life, sustained not by human effort but by divine presence and power.

We have never been closer to God than in that moment when we clung to Him with repentant hearts—when our minds, wills, and even the deepest affections of our souls turned from facing away from God to standing face-to-face with our Savior and our Lord. In an instant we went from distant to near. God regenerated our souls and made us alive in Christ Jesus. That miracle of new birth is captured with stunning clarity in Galatians 2:20:

> I have been crucified with Christ. It is no longer I who live, but Christ who lives in me. And the life I now live in the flesh I live by faith in the Son of God, who loved me and gave himself for me.

That's the moment everything changed. That's when we came alive. That's when we were brought near. That's when grace found us. That's when the with-God life began. Paul's words hint at what Scripture amplifies; "the life I now live" must be lived in our new birth posture of faith.

Newton's hymn reminds us that grace was never meant to stop at saving "a wretch like me." The grace that awakened us is the grace that walks with us through "many dangers, toils, and snares." The Christian life was always meant to be life with God, carried by His grace.

We wonder, why do some promises of Scripture feel elusive? Why does transformation seem inconsistent and powerless? Why does the Christian life so often feel like a cycle of effort and disappointment? Where is the abundant life Jesus came to give us?

Newton answers with stunning simplicity. "'Tis grace hath brought me safe thus far, and grace will lead me home." Scripture affirms the same reality. Paul writes in Titus 2:11–13,

> For the grace of God has appeared, bringing salvation for all people, training us to renounce ungodliness and worldly passions, and to live self-controlled, upright, and godly lives in the present age, waiting for our blessed hope, the appearing of the glory of our great God and Savior Jesus Christ.

Everything is right there. The grace that saved us is the grace that trains us. The same grace that brought us to life is the grace that teaches us how to live. The only way to renounce ungodliness, to live self-controlled and godly lives today is grace. That's it. It's not you. God's grace is truly amazing.

UNMERITED FAVOR *AND* UNLIMITED POWER

Before going any further, we need to be clear about what grace actually is. Over the years I have found it helpful to expand the common definition of grace into something more full-bodied and more reflective of what we see throughout Scripture. Grace is not only God's unmerited favor toward us; it is also His active power at work within us. Grace is His unmerited favor *and* unlimited power.

> The life of faith is not sustained by striving for God but by abiding with God.

That fuller understanding changes everything. Grace is not merely God's kindness, it is provision. Not only acceptance, but enablement. Not only rescue, but transformation power.

Early in my spiritual journey, my father, Joe Clauson, gave me a simple explanation of grace that has stayed with me ever since. He told me, "Grace is not permission to live as we like; it is the privilege to live as we never could before." He said it with passion. He believed it and lived it. Dad was describing exactly what Scripture reveals: Grace does not lower the standard of the Christian life—it supplies the power to live as we can't without it.

That kind of grace changes everything.

Yet many believers lean on strategies, disciplines, and sheer resolve, as if the Christian life were sustained by human determination. The result has been exhaustion among the people of God and a lingering sense that the life promised in Scripture remains just out of reach. But the gospel never taught us to take over where God left off.

Andrew Murray has been attributed with saying that God is ready to assume full responsibility for the life wholly yielded to Him. That is so spot on; it is rock-solid theological truth. The God who regenerates the human soul does not step back and ask us to manufacture transformation. He assumes responsibility for the life surrendered to Him.

A. W. Tozer put his finger directly on the answer: "God must do everything for us. Our part is to yield and trust."[3] Whenever we live as though growth depends primarily on our resolve, we quietly drift into that practical denial of the Christ who came to save us and lead us as the Good Shepherd. The unstoppable gospel is far greater than that.

Hudson Taylor gave us a taste of the spiritual fulcrum that changes everything when he said, "God's work done in *God's way* will never lack God's supply."[4] God's way is the with-God way. So consider with me that we may have leapt past the with-God life and adopted many good spiritual routines and activities that become empty, powerless, and quite frustrating.

BELOW THE WATERLINE

I was standing on an iceberg near Portage Glacier, just outside Anchorage, Alaska. This was years ago, back when massive chunks of ice broke away from the glacier and drifted close to shore. They looked solid—enormous, ancient, immovable. I had climbed out from the rocky beach and was hopping from one iceberg to the next, fascinated by their size and beauty, treating them almost like stepping stones. Each one felt firm beneath my boots. Stable. Safe.

Then a voice shattered the moment. "HEY! Be careful!" I turned toward the shore. A man was waving his arms, urgency written all over his face. "What you see above the water can flip and be underwater in a second!" he yelled. "Most of that iceberg is under the surface. If ice breaks underneath, the whole thing can flip in an instant."

I froze. Then slowly stepped back toward land. As I stood on the shore, I stared at those icebergs with new eyes. What looked massive and dependable above the surface was, in reality, only a fraction of the whole. Nearly 90 percent of an iceberg exists below the waterline—unseen, unexamined, and yet absolutely

> Without the practices that work beneath the surface, the visible disciplines slowly lose their power.

determinative of everything above it. A hidden fissure. A silent shift. And the entire iceberg could roll without warning.

That image has stayed with me ever since. Because it is not just true of glaciers. It is true of ships. It is true of leadership. And it is profoundly true of spiritual life. The unseen things often matter most, and what's below the surface can be seen in a heartbeat.

The great danger in the Christian life is not usually what we see. It is what we don't. It is living confidently above the waterline while neglecting what lies beneath the surface—assuming stability because what is visible appears strong. Scripture warns us repeatedly about this danger.

Richard Foster spoke of the *outward disciplines*—simplicity, submission, service—visible practices that express obedience and love.[5] Dallas Willard referred to these as the disciplines of *engagement*, the active ways we step into faithful living such as study, worship, celebration, service, prayer, and fellowship.[6] Scripture itself calls us to these practices. They matter. They are necessary.

But Foster and Willard were equally clear that the inner life must become the wellspring from which the outer life flows. And Willard carefully distinguished those outward disciplines from the disciplines of *abstinence*—solitude, silence, fasting, secrecy—practices that work beneath the surface, reordering the soul before God. Without them, the outward disciplines slowly lose their power. They remain visible, but they lack the stabilizing strength below the surface.

The problem is not that we practice outward disciplines. But the warning signs of fissures below the surface are when the outward disciplines feel mundane, empty, ritualistic, or obligatory. And that danger feels especially familiar. At least for me personally—and my suspicion after countless conversations with sincere, devoted followers of Jesus is that this is more collective than individual—we have often not lingered long enough below the waterline. We have not spent sustained time in the engine room of the spiritual life, where grace deepens, mercy reshapes, and the Spirit quietly does His transforming work. Instead, we move forward with what can be seen. Activity. Discipline. Ministry. Effort. Productivity. All good things. Necessary things. But insufficient things if they are not fueled by what happens beneath the surface in real communion with God.

Like those icebergs, what appears solid above the waterline can shift suddenly if there is a crack below it. We're only as strong above the surface with what people see as we are strong below the waterline. Unseen things matter most! The psalmist cried, "Deep calls to deep" (Ps. 42:7).

Every great ship reflects this reality. The towering structure above the surface—the decks, the masts, the bridge—captures our attention. But stability comes from below. The keel and the ballast lie hidden beneath the waterline, providing weight, balance, and direction. Without ballast below, no ship remains upright for long. Without depth beneath, it cannot endure the storms it is certain to face.

So it is with the life of faith. The Christian life was never meant to be powered primarily by the visible. It is fueled from below. Jesus said it plainly: "Abide in me, and I in you. . . . Apart from me you can do nothing" (John 15:4–5). That is a below-the-waterline truth.

Paul reminded us, "It is God who works in you, both to will and to work for his good pleasure" (Phil. 2:13). These are not surface-level realities. They describe the hidden, sustaining work of God beneath the visible life of obedience.

When we neglect that hidden life, the Christian life begins to feel heavy. Forced. Inconsistent. We push forward above the surface without sufficient ballast below it. We do and say the right things, maintain the right rhythms—yet something feels fragile. Vulnerable. One unseen crack, one unexpected pressure, and what appeared stable can begin to roll.

But when we linger below the waterline—when we give sustained attention to the inner life with God—everything changes. Grace flows more freely. Mercy reshapes us more deeply. Obedience becomes less about striving and more about responding. The outward disciplines regain their power because they are finally rooted in the inward reality of Christ at work within us.

This is the invitation before us. Not merely to refine what is visible. But to cultivate what is hidden. Not simply to polish what is above the surface. But to strengthen what lies beneath it. Because what is below the waterline will always determine everything above it.

A MOMENT OF CANDOR

Before we go any further, I need a moment of candor with you. For a lot of years, I spent my time managing the part of the iceberg that stuck out of the water. That's easy to do. Pretty quickly, the visible life becomes the only life you really know. It's not that you or I want to be inauthentic, but when what you constantly hear, whether spoken directly or simply implied, is that the Christian life revolves around a few key activities, it shapes you. Look right. Act right. Speak right. Stay morally clean. Produce results. Lead well. Maintain momentum. Be "on."

If you live that way long enough, you can begin to believe the Christian life exists primarily above the waterline.

And when that happens, it's possible to forget that the with-God life—the real life of faith—is lived mostly below the surface. Hidden. Quiet. Dependent. Relational. Sustained not by performance but by presence. We are far more dependent than we like to admit, and far more in need of nearness than our public lives often reveal.

I've been reminded of this by something as simple as watching Blaise, our husky. When he needs direction or senses uncertainty, he doesn't run off to prove himself. He presses close. He huddles near. He looks for protection and guidance. That posture is far closer to the with-God life than most of us experience.

What lies ahead in these pages is a journey below the waterline. I've not perfected this hidden life, but I am tasting and seeing that the Lord is good in ways that continually surprise and flood me with joy. When I meet with Him in the unseen disciplines, His gospel proves unstoppable. He never fails to meet me there. He reveals things in me I don't like, yet even that comes wrapped in mercy. He shows me a love unlike anything this world offers and fills my cup in ways that recalibrate everything. I find myself delighting more in the small things than the large ones. Even the visible roles I hold begin to lose their pull, not because they no longer matter, but because they are no longer the source of life. God's grace in the hidden places has a way of doing that.

So this is where we are now. We have come to the place where we can begin to go below the surface and watch God do something deep within us that we could never accomplish ourselves. The journey is humbling and freeing and quietly powerful. I'm grateful you've come this far, and where we're going next together will be nothing short of incredible.

The 30-Day With-God Challenge

Stop living *for* God while neglecting life *with* God. Spend the next 30 days learning how to walk closely with Jesus moment by moment throughout your day. Download this resource, print it out, and journal your responses to these 30 simple exercises and watch what God can do.

Unstoppablegospel.com/with

Part Three

UNLEASHING POWER

Chapter 7

UNSTOPPABLE LOVE

The smell hit me before I could even see it. The mess he was sitting in was horrific. Even before my eyes adjusted to the dim light, I knew what had happened. The cleanup was going to take a good bit of work.

"COME HERE," HE SAYS GENTLY

You've met Blaise, the husky pup I brought home from Alaska. Like many sled dogs, Blaise is genetically wired to run and comes from a long line of champions. He is a remarkable athlete. His body is built for endurance, for pulling, for covering mile after mile across frozen wilderness with astonishing speed and stamina.

But before any of that training can begin, something far more important has to happen. Bonding. Before the harness is fitted, before training miles are logged, before an Iditarod dog is prepared to cover over a thousand miles, there must be a close relationship built on trust and love. A sled dog does not run well for someone it doesn't know. The dog must learn the voice of the musher and determine whether he is safe. That kind of relationship does not happen automatically. It is built over time, and sometimes it is forged in moments you never expect.

One night when Blaise was about three months old, I woke up in the basement where I had been sleeping near him while he learned to relieve himself during the night. His small kennel sat only a few feet from my bed. If I heard rustling, that was the sign he needed to get up and out of the house.

This night it was different. I didn't hear anything, but the odor shocked my body to life. Without turning on the light, I slid out of bed and stepped toward him. As I got closer, the smell intensified. When I looked through dim light into the pen the scene confirmed what my nose had already told me. Blaise couldn't hold it. There was poop everywhere. Being a puppy, he had stepped in it repeatedly, spreading it across a folded blanket, up the sides of the pen, and all over himself. At some point he must have decided the situation was already beyond saving, because he had also peed all over the place. It was a complete disaster.

When he saw me standing there, his posture collapsed. His head dropped and his ears sank low. Little Blaise was so ashamed. In that moment I knew something important. The last thing he needed was a lecture or being yelled at. He knew he had messed up.

I sat down cross-legged on the basement floor and opened the door. Blaise didn't move or even look at me. I whispered his name and called him to me. Slowly he got up—one step and then another—he walked toward me hanging his head. He had never climbed into my lap before, and these were certainly not ideal conditions for our first attempt. But I felt Blaise needed some reassurance and care.

I said again quietly and gently, "Come up here, Blaise." With one slow-motion step he crawled into my lap. I knew what that meant for my jeans and shirt, but in that moment it was right. I wrapped my arms around him. The stench was awful—bad enough that I nearly dry-heaved—but I pulled him close and whispered into his ear, "I love you, buddy."

Something happened right there. Blaise melted into me. It was a strange bonding moment—sitting on a basement floor in the middle of the night holding a filthy puppy—but it changed something between us forever. From that night on, Blaise was close to me. He trusted me because he knew I loved him at his worst. In the middle of a poop and pee disaster Blaise felt my unconditional love. Our relationship would never be the same again.

That moment is a picture of the love of God. It illustrates truth that is hard to grasp. The love of God meets us in moments far messier than that kennel. The love of God meets us when our lives are a wreck. But it's the love of God that makes us run well this race of faith, and without it, we run out of duty or fear. Love conquers all!

INTO THE MESS

Anyone who has tasted salvation already knows the beginning of this story. You know what it is to have God move toward you before you ever move toward Him. You know how it feels to be invited in when you bring nothing but a mess.

Many people subconsciously assume that God waits for us to clean ourselves up before He moves toward us. It is insidious and one of the most subtle and dangerous lies Christ followers quietly carry. We assume that God's continued love depends on reasonable progress. Love holds as long as we keep our act together or at least show improvement.

But the unstoppable gospel reveals the exact opposite. God moves into our lives when we are anything but put together or cleaned up. He does not wait until we become lovable. He loves us first. Scripture says plainly, "We love because he first loved us" (1 John 4:19).

The initiative in salvation always belongs to God. Left to ourselves, we would never find our way to Him. Sin does not merely wound us; it blinds us. It bends our desires away from God and convinces us that independence from Him is freedom when in reality it is slavery. But freedom from spiritual slavery does not ensure lifelong victory. We will make a mess or two or many more. But God's love pursues us.

King David knew what it meant to discover the love of God in the middle of a devastating mess. After abusing his power to take Bathsheba, betraying one of his own loyal soldiers, and arranging the death of her husband, Uriah, to hide the sin, David eventually collapsed under the weight of his guilt. His cry of repentance in Psalm 51 reveals the brokenness of a man who finally saw the horror of what he had done:

> Have mercy on me, O God, according to your steadfast love; according to your abundant mercy blot out my transgressions.

David did not appeal to his past victories, his kingship, or his reputation. He appealed only to the steadfast love of God. The consequences of his sin were real and painful, and

Scripture does not minimize them. Yet even in the wake of one of the most vivid abuses of power recorded in Scripture, God's love still reached him. Grace did not erase the consequences, but it penetrated the darkness of David's failure and restored a broken man who had finally come to the end of himself—again.

> "There is more mercy in Christ than sin in us."

Into the mess explains how we are saved. But it also explains how we are changed. God's love is not reserved only for the moment of salvation. It remains present in the long and sometimes messy process of sanctification. We are not only loved when we are forgiven, we are loved while we are being changed. Love always breaks through our shame and mess and calls us closer.

Anyone who has walked with Jesus for very long knows the temptation to not be honest with God about our failures. There are moments when you look at your life and wonder how you could possibly have made the same mess again. After all God has done for you, after all the ways He has changed you, you still find yourself staring at the wreckage of something you have done or neglected. In those moments you often hang your head, as Blaise did that night in the kennel. You quietly wonder how God who chose you could still love you. And Satan and his demons whisper lies in the dark that God doesn't love you or that you better clean it up before you lift your head up.

Yet it is often in those very moments that the love of God becomes most clear. God does not wait for the mess to be cleaned up before He draws near. Again and again, He steps right into it. As the great Puritan Richard Sibbes famously wrote, "There is more mercy in Christ than sin in us."[1] That truth means that even when you find yourself standing in the mess with your head down, the heart of God is calling you—"come here."

LOVE ABSORBS THE COST

The moment I saw my husky pup stepping toward me with paws filled with chunks of poop, mixed with fresh urine and a combination of both matted into his hair . . . I knew I was about to pay a price here. I was going to wear it and clean it up.

But what a small comparison to the love and grace of God. Real love absorbs the cost. Blaise couldn't clean it up, so it was all on me. I picked him up, wiped him down, scrubbed the floor, and changed my clothes. He didn't fix what he had done—I carried the burden of it so things could be made right again.

That small moment is a faint picture of what happened at the cross. Scripture says, "He himself bore our sins in his body on the tree" (1 Peter 2:24). But does He still bear our sins after months or decades of our following Jesus and messing up? Four times the New Testament uses a powerful word and theologians love to discuss it—*propitiation*. It simply means that Jesus absorbed the full cost of sin. Past sin. Present sin. Future sin. The justice of God that should have fallen on us fell on Jesus instead. Charles Spurgeon said it clearly: "Christ has taken the whole of your sin, past, present, and to come, and has borne the punishment for it all."[2]

Love like that does not make a believer want to wander into sin. It does the opposite. That kind of love becomes the catalyst to live a life we never imagined possible.

I learned a small glimpse of that kind of love long before I understood the cross. There were seasons when I was far from God and making a mess of my life. More than once, my dad stepped in and bailed me out, with a ride or a place to sleep and carried the pain of a son who lived reckless without yelling, mocking, or scolding me . . . he just loved me. The love got tough from Dad, but it was always with a tear that showed me he hated my pain but loved me enough to let me sit in it. He absorbed costs he didn't create and paid with his time what he didn't owe. And strangely, it didn't leave me feeling crushed by shame; it compelled me to change. When someone loves you like that, you don't want to keep making the same mess—you want to live differently.

And that's exactly how love works in us even after we come to Christ. As Jerry Bridges wisely said,

> Your worst days are never so bad that you are beyond the reach of God's grace. And your best days are never so good that you are beyond the need of God's grace.[3]

The gospel tells us that our sin was far worse than we ever wanted to admit—and Christ is a far greater Savior than we ever imagined. On the cross He did not minimize our mess. He absorbed it. And that kind of love changes everything.

LOVE HOLDS

In our family we've built a tradition. Whenever we're saying goodbye to someone we won't be seeing for a while, I'll say, "Bring it in." And everyone knows what that means—group hug. Arms go around shoulders, we pull in close, and on the count of three everyone squeezes toward the center. I've even done it with small groups of people before gatherings—"Bring it in, group hug." And suddenly there's laughter, shoulders pressed together, people leaning in.

There's something deeply bonding about that moment. Because we were built for it. And that leads to something I want

> When you begin to see the kind of love that refuses to abandon you even at your worst, it awakens something powerful inside.

to say to you. I want to talk especially to the people who feel like they're not supposed to need that kind of affection. Many times, that lands hardest on men, though women can feel it too. Many believe strength means holding everything inside. Women and men today are often whispered something from the thief and accuser: *You're too accomplished to cry. Too strong to break down. Too put together to need a hug.* Nothing could be further from the truth.

We've lived with such a distorted sense of strength that we hardly allow ourselves to believe in love that holds on. Somewhere along the way we started thinking real maturity means pushing through pain and pretending everything is fine. But that kind of toughness is often just bravado or pain covering insecurity.

There is nothing weak about crawling into the arms of God and pouring out your heart. There is something profoundly right about resisting the temptation to grit your teeth and instead letting God hear you. Letting Him speak into your heart when He says, "Bring it in." And lingering there.

That's where real strength is born. The affection of God is profound, and He delights to pour it into the lives of His children. The love of God does not merely forgive us; it transforms us.

Transformation in the life of a disciple comes through an encounter with the living, loving God. When His love meets you in the very place of your failure—when it cuts straight through the layers of shame you wish you could hide behind—it does not crush you; it restores you. The love of God reaches into the places we most want to conceal, lifts our heads, steadies our hearts, and reminds us that we are still His. And when you begin to see that kind of love—love that refuses to abandon you even at your worst—it awakens something powerful inside. Your heart begins to soften, your affection for Him deepens, and slowly, unmistakably, you begin to resemble the One who has loved you so fiercely.

Another quiet fear many Christ followers carry is the fear that they will not make it to the end. They worry that their faith might fail or that their weaknesses might eventually overwhelm them. But Scripture speaks with remarkable clarity about the permanence of God's love. Read Paul's ringing words from Romans 8:38–39 (NIV):

> Neither death nor life, neither angels nor demons, neither the present nor the future, nor any powers, neither height nor depth, nor anything else in all creation, will be able to separate us from the love of God that is in Christ Jesus our Lord.

When Blaise looked up at me from my lap and into my eyes, there was almost a look of bewilderment—like he couldn't quite understand that I still loved him at his worst. It was a beautiful moment. As Martyn Lloyd-Jones once observed, "The ultimate test of our spirituality is the measure of our amazement at the grace of God."[4] The same love that pursues you in the mess is the love that holds you afterward—be amazed.

AS YOU ARE

Some lessons I keep learning even after forty years. It's hard to believe that for four decades I've had the privilege of serving as a pastor. But the greatest joy hasn't been preaching sermons or leading ministries. The greatest joy has been experiencing personally what I invite others to taste and see. And it's an amazing thing. I can hardly put words to it. *Flummoxed* may be the best word I know—those moments when I pause long enough to let God see me thoroughly as I am. In those quiet places He cuts through my walls of resistance and lets me see again that although He is God and I am not, He loves me still.

There have been early mornings when my soul was shaking its head, almost in disbelief, whispering, *How could You love me, God?* I've had moments when the weight of my own shortcomings seemed painfully clear. And yet there He is—steady, patient, unhurried—saying, *Come here, Karl.* And the remarkable thing is that the same invitation is extended to you.

Come as you are.

You may have come to believe that you are a disappointment to God. Maybe you've tried to grow and failed. You might wonder "How could He possibly love me?" when you have fought the same sins again and again. You may look at other Christ followers and assume they must have something you do not. Somewhere along the way you have quietly begun to believe that God must be done with you. But the remarkable truth about the love of God is that it sees the mess of your life clearly and still moves toward you.

The invitation is simply this: Come. Come honestly. Come with the mess. Come with the shame. Come with the failures you cannot seem to overcome. Come with the parts of your life you wish no one else could see. Jesus did not say, "Fix yourself and then follow me." He said, "Come to me, all who labor and are heavy laden, and I will give you rest" (Matt. 11:28). The love of God does not begin when you finally get your life together or even get past your shame. It begins the moment you come—with your failures and your shame. Love feels best when shame seems to have consumed us and then through God's love shame is washed away.

And from that love—from the unstoppable love of God—transformation begins again. Once you experience that love, something remarkable happens. You begin to breathe, live, and dream again.

What God Says About You Matters Most

The devil and demonic forces want you trapped in shame, fear, and false identity. Download and learn how to live fully confident of how deeply loved you are by God. Knowing what He calls you, how He sees you, and where He wants to take you will provide the spiritual fuel for following Jesus.

Unstoppablegospel.com/identity

Chapter 8

UNSTOPPABLE SURRENDER

I was arrested once when I was running from God. I was a reckless young man—unmoored, untethered, drifting without any real relationship with Him. I spent one long night at the Fisherman's Bar in Naknek, Alaska, and if drinking wasn't foolish enough, the way I drank made me dangerous to myself and others. It was like there was a hole in me I kept trying to fill, and the more I poured in, the emptier I became. Alcohol didn't help me in any way—it just lowered the guardrails until I started doing things a sober Karl never would have done.

IT'S TIME

What I remember next comes in fragments. It was late—early morning, really. The front desk at the little hotel was shut down.

I must have been looking for a room, or at least a place to land after the bar shut down. I remember being in that narrow hallway, quiet, dim, the kind of silence that only comes in those in-between hours of the night. I knocked on a door. No answer. And then, in a moment that still makes me wince with embarrassment, I threw my shoulder into it. The jamb splintered. The door gave way. I stumbled in and lay down on the bed.

I woke up hours later with sunlight cutting through the window. For a moment I didn't know where I was. Then it all came flooding back—the door, the damage, the night. I sat on that bed, the heaviness of it all settling in, and I felt sick. Deep down, even far from God, I knew better. I had been raised better. I now just wanted to make it right. My hope was that no one knew yet what I'd done. I figured I'd go get some cash to pay for the damage and the room, and quietly resolve this debacle. But they knew. They were just too afraid of me to come in and tell me I owed them, so they called the police.

I slipped out the back and was walking to the bank when the lone squad car in that small Alaskan town pulled up behind me. The lights weren't flashing, but the moment was unmistakable. The officer stepped out, looked at me, and said, "Put your hands in the air." And I did. Even now, I can feel the weight of that moment—the sobriety of it, the humbling reality of standing there exposed with nothing to hide behind. My hands were raised. Empty. In that instant, everything comes into sharp focus. You realize how vulnerable you are, how quickly things could go another way. If I had lifted those hands holding anything—anything at all—it could have been misunderstood in a second. But I stood there with nothing, and off to the jail I went—fingerprinting, rights read, bail made.

As soon as I could, I went straight back to that hotel. I apologized—genuinely—and I paid far more than it would cost to fix the door and cover the room. I just wanted to make it right. Those were hard days, and it wasn't long after that—just a few short years—that God came near and made something unmistakably clear: It's time to surrender. And surrender is a brutally hard thing, because it forces you to face the truth that what you've been holding on to—what you've been gripping with everything you've got—is not giving you life. Whether it's a bottle, the wheel of a new car, a loaded 401(k), a thriving business, or a position that makes you feel secure; none of it can save you. And then, in mercy, God comes close and says, put your hands in the air—let it go.

Surrender is not a one and done. It is the ongoing invitation of the Holy Spirit, not just before your life is transformed, but every single day after. I don't know how many times I've had to surrender over the last four decades, but I can tell you this—there have been days when it's happened more than once in a single day. Because you cannot follow Jesus until you lay something down, and you cannot follow Him for salvation or for sanctification while still clinging to what cannot save you. Surrender is deeply personal—it's between you and God—and you know exactly what it is He's asking you to release.

In the shallow version of Christianity we've often settled for, we've tried to live with one hand raised to God while the other grips tightly to the things of this world, but it doesn't work. You can't lift your hands to God in surrender while holding on to anything else. And here's the paradox—the beautiful, unstoppable reality of it all: When your hands are in the air, gripping nothing, you finally discover that you have everything.

EMPTY-HANDED

One of the great joys of my life was speaking to a few thousand people at a church in Scottsdale, Arizona, and at the end of the message I invited them to do something together that most of us would feel uncomfortable doing alone. As the worship team played their instruments in what would be a concluding song, I invited the audience to raise their hands. I explained that the universal sign of surrender—no matter where you are in the world—is hands in the air with nothing in them, because if someone holds a gun or a knife to your back, instinct takes over and your hands go up empty. But here's the irony—it's also the universal sign of victory, because when an athlete crosses the finish line, whether in first place or simply having pushed through to the finish of a grueling marathon, their hands go up empty, and so raised, empty hands become the symbol of both surrender and victory, which makes it one of the most beautiful postures in the world: to stand before God empty-handed.

And I will never forget what happened next, because as those hands began to rise across the auditorium—row after row, person after person—it was amazing to witness what a few thousand empty-handed people did before God, and it was not just a gesture but something sacred, holy, because you could sense that God was dealing with souls all across that auditorium in a deeply personal and powerful way, bringing things to the surface that needed to be laid down that very day, whether it was sin, control, fear, shame, or a future someone was clinging to, and in that moment surrender and victory were happening at the same time across a sea of lifted, empty hands.

The danger, however, is that many of us begin that way—we come to Jesus empty-handed—but somewhere along the way we start picking things back up, and we end up self-sabotaging our relationship with Him by trying to hold on to Jesus while also holding on to everything else, even though those very things must go if we are to experience restored joy and the fullness of the life He has for us. You see this pattern all throughout Scripture, because no one takes hold of Jesus without first laying something down. Simon and Andrew left their nets, Abraham laid down his homeland, his future, and ultimately Isaac, Moses laid down royal privilege and comfort, Matthew left behind a lucrative but corrupt career, Paul relinquished his status, reputation, and self-made righteousness, the woman at the well laid down her shame and isolation, and Zacchaeus laid down his greed by giving generously and making restitution. What becomes unmistakably clear is that no one takes hold of Jesus without letting go of something or someone.

> Raised empty hands become the symbol of both surrender and victory, which makes it one of the most beautiful postures in the world: to stand before God empty-handed.

And the battle does not end there. Surrender is a daily invitation of the Holy Spirit to release whatever is competing with Christ for our hearts, which is why Tim Keller said:

> An idol is anything more important to you than God, anything that absorbs your heart and imagination more than God, anything you seek to give you what only God can give.[1]

So it is right for us to pause and ask honestly whether we are self-sabotaging our relationship with Jesus by trying to take hold of all that He is and all that He offers without laying something down, because if we are clinging to control, comfort, security, an unhealthy relationship, secret sin, hidden addiction, approval, reputation, success, money, a carefully scripted future, bitterness, unforgiveness, pride, fear, our image, or our independence, then those things are standing in the way of what God wants to give.

This is exactly what the apostle Paul came to understand in Philippians 3, because he had every reason to cling to his background, his achievements, his religious status, and his moral record, but after encountering Christ he came to see all of it differently—listing his achievements of this world and then declaring, "Indeed, I count everything as loss because of the surpassing worth of knowing Christ Jesus my Lord . . . and count them as rubbish, in order that I may gain Christ" (Phil. 3:8). This is the language of a man who has opened his hands and let everything go so that he might take hold of what truly matters.

And that is the great paradox of the Christian life, because you cannot hold on to anything and take hold of Jesus at the same time. Nothing but laying down someone or something will free your hands to take hold of Christ. But when you come to Him empty-handed, you discover something stunning; that in letting go of what you thought you needed, you receive what you were truly made for, and when your hands are in the air gripping nothing, you finally realize that you have everything.

THE SURPRISE OF SURRENDER

Whatever we lay down, whenever we come empty-handed before God, He fills us up. We don't surrender to get, but we do surrender to receive more of Him. And yet surrender can feel like the least logical, even the most insane thing we could do in a given moment, because whatever we're holding on to is doing something for us. It's propping us up, numbing a pain, quieting a fear, medicating a wound, giving us a sense of control, identity, or relief, even if it's temporary. It may not be that satisfying, but it feels like something, and letting go of that something can feel like stepping into nothing. That's what makes surrender so hard—it feels like loss when everything in the kingdom says it's actually gain.

The story about Elijah and a widow in Zarephath captures this tension perfectly. She was living in the midst of a severe famine with nothing left but a handful of flour and a little oil—just enough, in her mind, for one final meal before she and her son would die. That's the moment God steps in. Elijah meets her as she's gathering sticks, and he asks her for water, then adds something even more staggering—"Bring me a piece of bread." She tells him plainly that she has almost nothing left, but Elijah presses in with a promise from God: If she would give first, the flour and oil would not run out.

Somehow, in that moment, she believed God. She took a risk and crossed the threshold of faith. She opened her hands and gave what little she had left. Scripture captures the immediate result of her surrender with stunning simplicity.

> She and he and her household ate for many days. The jar of flour was not spent, neither did the jug of oil become empty, according to the word of the Lord that he spoke by Elijah. (1 Kings 17:15–16)

What followed was not a one-time miracle, but a daily, sustaining provision. Day after day, meal after meal, the flour did not run out, and the oil did not fail. God didn't just meet her need once—He sustained her through the entire famine. And as if that weren't enough, later in the story when her son became deathly ill and stopped breathing, God used Elijah to bring him back to life, restoring not just her provision but her future.

The surprise of surrender. That's the truth of this passage—God rewards empty hands. Not because we give to get, and not because we humble ourselves to be lifted up as some kind of transaction, but because it is simply how His kingdom works. Every time we let go of what we're clinging to, God gives something better—something deeper, something lasting, something more like Him.

Every time we let go of what we're clinging to, God gives something better—deeper, lasting, something more like Him.

The story of one widow in Zarephath is a story of surrender—and the surprise that follows it. The tendency for all of us is to know, at some level, that we need to come empty-handed before the Lord. There are things we need to give Him, things we must surrender. But crossing that threshold—actually letting go, actually believing that God will meet us there without trying to control what He gives in return—that requires faith. And even that faith is a gift from God.

But just consider this for a moment: What might God give you if you dared to believe Him? If you came with a surrendered heart and open hands, laying down that thing—whatever that thing is—what might He do? Because the promise woven all throughout Scripture is this: Whatever God gives will be abundantly greater than what you were holding on to.

LETTING GO

Early in the mornings, I have time alone with God. I'll speak more about this later in "Unstoppable Examination," but most mornings there is something God brings to the surface. It usually starts in the closest circles of my life—my bride, the way I'm treating her, the way I'm leading her, what it really means for me to love her as Christ loved the church—and almost without exception, it requires me to lay something down. When I take hold of anything that is not from God, I find it impossible to do His will until I lay that thing down. It's amazing what we can take hold of without even realizing it; subtle desires for recognition, a quiet craving for security in the work we do, a need to be seen, to be affirmed. But God, in His kindness, keeps putting His finger on those things and saying, *let it go*. And then there are the private things, the ones no one else sees, but you do. You and your loving Father do. And if you'll listen closely, you can hear Him whisper, *lay it down. There's something more ahead.*

One of the most brutal things I ever had to let go of was a dream. It wasn't just any dream, it was something that had taken root deep in my heart. I had a vision that every person in the state of Alaska would get a fair shot at the gospel, that there would be life offered in Christ for every Alaskan. I shared that vision with thousands of people, and we were in it together. It felt alive. It felt right. And then, in what seemed like a moment, I was confronted over things that needed to change in me. It was the first time I had heard something in me that needed to change, but I was ultimately grateful to hear what was said to me. But the dream of bringing the gospel to every Alaskan seemingly vanished. I was in a season of relational and vocational challenges, dealing with motives and actions of others I couldn't control. I was asked to remain in my current position, but the conditions were untenable.

It was confusing. It felt unjust. And it was deeply painful. There are moments when you let something go, and then there are moments when God has to pry it from your fingers, and this was one of those moments. I didn't want to release it, but over time, it was surrendered.

Years passed, and I found myself thousands of miles away from any possibility of that dream, the gospel for every Alaskan becoming reality, or so I thought. Then God opened a door for me to serve as a morning host with Moody Radio in Chicago. The Lord gave our team favor—real, unmistakable favor—and after several years, I was told that our show was going to expand to a much broader platform. I had no idea what that meant at the time.

> God is never taking something from you without doing something deeper, wiser, and more enduring through it.

But then I learned something that stopped me dead in my tracks. Of the roughly sixty stations that would now carry the broadcast, thirteen of them were in Alaska. In that moment, my heart just about leapt out of my chest. My mind went straight back to that dream—the gospel for every Alaskan, life in Christ for every Alaskan—and now, through those antennas scattered across that vast and rugged land, the message of Jesus was reaching places I could have never touched on my own. Out of all the stations across North America, the highest concentration was in the very place I had once carried so deep in my heart.

Even now, there are moments when I'm live on the air—reading Scripture, calling people to repentance, inviting them to follow Jesus—and it hits me. What I once thought was gone, what I once had to lay down, God has returned in a way I never could have orchestrated. Not by my strength or strategy. But by His hand.

That's the nature of surrender. It rarely makes sense in the moment. It often feels like loss. But God is never taking something from you without doing something deeper, wiser, and more enduring through it. The apostle Paul understood this when he looked back on everything he once held dear and counted it all as loss compared to knowing Christ. What he laid down seemed significant in the moment, but what God gave him in return echoes into eternity. His life became a living testimony that surrender is not the end of something—it's the beginning of something far greater.

I don't know what you're holding on to today, friend, but I know this—God is good, His Word is true, and when He asks you to lay something down, it's never to diminish your life but to deepen it. That's the God of unstoppable surrender. That's the God of surprise. And that's the God who is gently, persistently, lovingly asking you to let it go.

Four Steps to Freedom

Discover the freedom of laying down the very things that are holding you back. Download this survey of Scripture for those substitute gods that we need to let go of. This biblical pathway to freedom will be an ongoing resource as you walk with Jesus. Surrender is the pathway of spiritual liberty.

Unstoppablegospel.com/surrender

Chapter 9

UNSTOPPABLE EXAMINATION

Her phone ringing wasn't unusual, but when my bride of thirty-five years told me who was calling, everything in me froze. You don't want your doctor calling you late Friday night. Just a few weeks earlier, Junanne's general practitioner had suggested a CT scan of her abdomen. It felt precautionary at the time, routine and nothing urgent. But now, sitting across from her at dinner, just minutes after we had walked out of a movie and were settling in to finish our date with a good meal, everything shifted. She stepped away to take the call in a quieter place, and I sat there staring at my entrée—I couldn't touch it. My appetite vanished, and my mind didn't drift, it sprinted. Deep down, I already knew. I knew the news was not good.

About ten minutes later, Junanne returned, the doctor still on the line. "She wants to talk with you, Bub," she said with a resolute but gentle voice. My hand was shaking as I stood up and walked out into the lobby, pressing the phone to my ear. And there it was, the words no husband ever wants to hear. The scan had revealed what was undeniable—two significant masses. The likely diagnosis was ovarian cancer.

SUBTLE SYMPTOMS

When you love someone as deeply as I love my bride, it feels like the world stops. Not just slows but stops entirely. And the pain I felt in that moment was not for myself; it was for her. My bride is a quiet woman but filled with indomitable strength; unyielding, resilient, and steady. In the weeks that followed, I watched her face this storm with a quiet courage that still humbles me. I remember her shedding a single tear as we silently came back to our home and faced the future. One tear, and that was it.

God, in His kindness, led us to a remarkable surgeon at the University of Chicago, a teaching physician who had performed thousands of these procedures. We gathered people who committed to pray and my wife felt like she was in a bubble of peace. Still, I had read the statistics, and I knew the odds. Given the size of the tumors, my expectations were not good. But I followed the courageous faith of Junanne and had confidence in God, and we prayed with faith, believing God could heal.

The day of surgery came, and I went with her to the hospital, sitting alone in one of those small waiting rooms reserved for families walking through life-altering moments. I prayed, not casually or passively, but with intensity, pleading with God to heal my bride. Time stretched in a way that made every minute feel like an hour. Then I heard footsteps in the hallway, and when the door opened, the doctor walked in and told me there was indeed cancer, but it was some of the most encapsulated cancer he had ever seen. He explained that his hope was that nothing had escaped and nothing had spread. Sixteen or more biopsies were taken, and not one of them showed any trace of cancer beyond those two large tumors.

Then came the waiting. Ovarian cancer has a critical two-year window, and if you can make it through that period, the survival rate rises dramatically, almost indistinguishable from anyone else walking down the street. Those two years were not easy, but I will never forget the moment we crossed that threshold. The doctor looked at us and said that based on everything he could see, both inside and out, Junanne was cancer-free. She remains cancer-free to this day, now nearly five years later.

What strikes me most as I look back is that we could not see it. When those tumors were growing, we could not see them. There were only subtle symptoms, small things that prompted a closer look. That was it. Without the help of technology, we would have kept right on living our daily life until my bride's life was cut short.

And that is where this begins to turn, because unstoppable examination is an unseen discipline. It is private, personal, and deeply intimate. It is you and God, with no audience and no performance. It is the intentional invitation we extend to Him to search us, examine us, and show us what we cannot see. The reason we must do this is because we are remarkably poor at diagnosing ourselves. My wife ignored her doctor's first request to get a CT scan after a few small symptoms. It wasn't until the doctor asked again for her to get the scan that we got on the schedule. We assume we are healthy, we convince ourselves we are fine, and we manage surface symptoms while missing deeper realities.

Spiritually speaking, we often carry things beneath the surface—patterns, motives, and compromises—that go undetected because we have stopped looking or perhaps never truly started. Without examination, those things do not remain neutral; they grow quietly beneath the surface, shaping us in ways we do not fully understand and often stealing life out from under us. While they may not ultimately destroy us, they will certainly hinder us, keeping us from the fullness and abundance that God intends for us to experience.

SEEING OURSELVES RIGHTLY

We think we see ourselves rightly. We assume we can see ourselves clearly, accurately, honestly—but we don't, and we can't. That may be hard to hear, but it is one of the most powerful truths I could ever offer you, and one I can testify has been among the most transformational realities in my own life over the past five years. If you can, even for a moment, embrace the reality that you are not a reliable evaluator of your own heart, you will place yourself in a position of profound spiritual advantage.

We see glimpses of this limitation in the ordinary moments of life. A coworker expresses hurt over something we never intended, and we are caught off guard. Our spouse shares how our words or actions landed, and we quietly realize we are not the husband or wife we thought we were. Our children, whether in passing comments or honest conversations, reveal blind spots in how we raised them, and we begin to recognize that we have things to confess and make right. Even in childhood, many of us first encountered this reality in something as simple as a parent-teacher conference, where an honest student might actually internalize, *I don't see myself as clearly as I thought I did.* The evidence is everywhere. Left to ourselves, we consistently overestimate our health and underestimate our unhealthiness.

When David says, "Search me," he is inviting God to sift through every layer of his heart.

This is why one of the most courageous prayers in all of Scripture is found in Psalm 139:23–24, where David cries out, "Search me, O God, and know my heart! Try me and know my thoughts! And see if there be any grievous way in me, and lead me in the way everlasting!"

This is not a casual prayer; it is a bold and vulnerable invitation. This is manhood at its finest, not bravado or self-sufficiency, but a humble invitation for God to take a look. It reveals a depth of relationship with God that few of us consistently exercise, a willingness to be fully known because we trust the One who knows us.

There is an important contextual note here. Psalm 139 is widely understood to have been written during a mature season of David's life, likely after many of his greatest failures, including his sin with Bathsheba. In fact, David wrote Psalm 51 just after being confronted by Nathan about his moral disaster. In verse 6 you can see a significant shift in David's self-awareness when he wrote to God, "Behold, you delight in truth in the inward being, and you teach me wisdom in the secret heart." David learned in a moral crisis that he didn't know himself as well in the "secret" places as he thought. By the time David wrote Psalm 139, it reflects a man who has come to terms with both the depth of God's knowledge and the depth of his own need. He is no longer posturing. He is not defending himself. The verbs in this closing prayer are not hypothetical or distant; they are immediate, urgent, and ongoing.

When David says, "Search me," he is not asking for a surface-level review. He is inviting God to dig all the way down into him, to leave nothing unexamined, to sift through every layer of his heart. When he says, "Know me," he is not merely requesting observation; he is asking God to move beyond behavior into the motives and desires that drive his life. It is as if David is saying, "God, don't just evaluate what I do—understand why I do it. Trace the roots beneath my actions and expose what is really there."

Then David continues, "See if there be any grievous way in me." This is a plea for identification, for God to look and reveal anything within him that is offensive, harmful, distorted, or out of alignment with His ways. It is an open-hearted request: "Show me what I cannot see, even if it is painful to face." The phrase carries the sense of anything that causes harm, not only to others but also to his own soul, anything that leads him down a path of destruction rather than life.

And then come the remarkable closing words: "Lead me in the way everlasting." This is not merely a request for correction but for direction. David is asking God to guide him onto a path that is enduring, ancient, and life-giving, a path that stands in contrast to the fleeting and deceptive ways of the world. "Everlasting" here carries the sense of something that is rooted, established, and aligned with God's eternal purposes. It is a request not just to be shown what is wrong, but to be led into what is right, what lasts, what truly gives life.

Theologians across generations have recognized the depth of this prayer. Charles Spurgeon once wrote, "The prayer is an appeal to God to be the judge of the man, and to search him as none but God can search him."[1] And Augustine of Hippo captured the heart of it when he said, "Let me know myself, O Lord, and know You; for in knowing You, I shall rightly know myself."[2] Each of these voices points to the same reality: Left to ourselves, we remain hidden from ourselves, but before God, nothing remains concealed.

The invitation is unmistakably clear through the life of David. Do not settle for what others see, and certainly do not settle for what you think you see. Go to the One who sees everything. He may reveal that by His grace you are healthier than you feared. But He may also uncover things beneath the surface that require real attention and honest repentance. Without that level of examination, the consequences are not small. Spiritually speaking, we begin to wither. The promises of God remain just out of reach, not because they are unavailable, but because we have not allowed Him to deal with what is in the way.

This kind of examination requires a level of honesty that many of us have never fully embraced. It asks us to lay down self-protection, to release control, and to trust God with what we would rather keep hidden. But to be led in the way everlasting—that is a goal worthy of any cost.

TASTE AND SEE

"Oh, taste and see that the Lord is good" (Ps. 34:8). In their classic Old Testament commentary,[3] Carl Friedrich Keil and Franz Delitzsch emphasize that the invitation to "taste and see that the Lord is good" calls God's children to a real and experiential knowledge of God's goodness, not merely an abstract or theoretical acknowledgment. The psalm directs the godly to *prove God's goodness in lived experience*, so that it becomes personally known rather than merely conceived intellectually. They invite the

> What keeps us from tasting? Pride tells us we're already fine. Fear whispers that if God really looks, He'll find too much.

reader beyond theory into encounter. This is not an invitation to analyze God's goodness, but to step into it—to experience it, to know it firsthand.

That kind of tasting—especially when it comes to honest communication from God through the power of the Holy Spirit—is, in many ways, an acquired taste. It doesn't always feel natural at first. I heard what blue cheese was before I tasted it and that was a problem. It seems like a prank the first time you're invited to try it. Mold? Really? And yet, over time, what once repelled you becomes something you actually enjoy or crave.

So it is with the voice of God in deep, personal examination. Keil and Delitzsch are pointing to something experiential. This "taste" is not passive. It requires engagement. It invites you to step forward and experience what cannot be understood from a distance. And when it comes to unstoppable examination, this is exactly what is happening. God is not inviting you into cold scrutiny, but into a living encounter with His goodness—even in the places where He searches you most deeply.

This is what we must understand: unstoppable examination is not about exposure for exposure's sake; it is about discovering that God is good, even as He presses in and we feel the sting. The challenge is that this kind of examination is so personal, so thorough, and so unknown that you cannot anticipate what will be revealed. There is no way to know what you do not know. But without taking a bite—without stepping into this—we will miss the taste of being led in the way everlasting.

So what keeps us from tasting? Pride tells us we're already fine. Fear whispers that if God really looks, He'll find too much. Self-sufficiency convinces us we can manage our own lives. Busyness keeps us distracted enough to avoid reflection. Shame tells us we're better off not knowing. And unfamiliarity makes this whole idea feel strange and uncomfortable. Sociologists and theologians alike would agree—these forces combine to keep us at a distance from the very thing our souls most need. But the invitation still stands: taste and see.

I think about my granddaughter, Baby Kate, just beginning to explore solid foods. It is one of the most fun things to watch. She approaches each new bite with curiosity, a touch of hesitation, and then wonder. Some first bites she spits out. But when it's tasty, she puts it in her mouth, pauses, and then her face lights up as if to say, "Wow . . . this is new . . . and this is good." There is no overthinking, no resistance, just discovery. She doesn't know what she's been missing until she tastes it, and once she does, everything changes.

That is the invitation before us. Not to stand back and analyze, but to step in and experience. Because on the other side of that first bite—honest, Spirit-led examination—is the unmistakable realization that what God offers is not only true, but deeply, undeniably good. I'll admit, some first bites from God are an acquired taste, but everything He offers us is ultimately good.

FIVE MINUTES THAT WILL CHANGE YOUR LIFE

Five years ago, I began a spiritual discipline that has become one of those deep-water, below-the-surface, unstoppable practices in my life: the discipline of examination. It is not complicated, but it is profoundly transformational.

This is how it goes. The first thing I do when I get up in the morning is head downstairs and pour a cup of coffee—black, no sugar, no cream, just the way God made it. Then I head down another level into our living room and settle into a leather glider. I set the coffee beside me, and as it begins to cool, I take a sip and simply begin, "Okay, here we are again, Father. Search me, O God, and know my heart; try me and know my thoughts, and see if there be any grievous way in me, and lead me in the way everlasting." And then I listen.

I will speak more to the power of the Spirit later, but I can tell you this: The Holy Spirit has never failed me yet. God gave us His Son, and the words of Jesus—what James calls the perfect law—are what we are invited to look intently into. The whole of Scripture becomes the instrument, and the Spirit of God faithfully brings truth to mind, looking into the places where it is needed most. What begins as five minutes often stretches—ten, fifteen, sometimes twenty or even thirty—as the conversation deepens and clarity comes.

What surfaces most often are the spheres of relationship in my life. God has a way of working in concentric circles, starting closest to home and moving outward. Again and again, I am brought back to loving my wife, to live with her in an understanding way so my prayers will not be hindered (1 Peter 3:7). Sometimes God says, "Fold the laundry she asked you to fold yesterday." Often God asks me to listen more carefully so Junanne feels heard. Other times it is the quiet conviction not to try to shape her into my image, but to love her for who she is. The clarity of God speaking when invited is striking. It is not vague or abstract; it is direct and unmistakable.

> Ask Him to lead you, not just away from what is wrong, but toward what is right.

From there, the Spirit often moves outward into my relationships with those I work with and minister alongside. I am prompted to consider how to love them well, how to keep unnecessary pressure off, how to affirm more intentionally, and where course corrections are needed, more gently. At times I am led to recognize the need for an apology, words that were poorly chosen, attitudes that were misaligned.

There are also moments when deeper things surface about me that no one knows, and I often don't either until God shows me. Areas I might be inclined to overlook or keep hidden, subtle idols that have taken root or patterns that have gone unaddressed. These are the things that, left alone, would remain beneath the surface. Like my bride's cancer symptoms; if ignored, the tumors of spiritual sickness will only grow. But when God is invited to search, to know, and to reveal, nothing stays concealed. And what is no longer concealed can be healed.

It is remarkable how clear God is when you ask Him to do this. There are often things I may have sensed in passing, quick impressions I could easily dismiss or move past, but in this space of intentional examination, they come into focus. That is the power of this practice. What you cannot see on your own, God is faithful to show you. All it takes is an invitation.

I invite you now! Wherever you are, no matter what time of day it is, would you take five minutes? Just five. Sit down, quiet your heart, and ask God honestly, "What do You see that I don't see?" And when He reveals it—and He will—own it. Not as your identity, but as something to bring into the light. Agree with

Him. That is what confession is: saying the same thing about it that God says. And then ask Him to lead you, not just away from what is wrong, but toward what is right, toward what is lasting.

This is not complicated, but it is costly. It requires humility and honesty, a willingness to be known. But this is where transformation begins, where the unseen work of God reshapes the visible parts of your life. This is where the gospel moves from something you believe to something you experience. So take five minutes. Invite Him in, listen carefully, respond humbly, and walk forward in obedience. And He will undoubtedly lead you in the way everlasting.

The Best Five Minutes of Your Day

Slow down and invite God to reveal what may be shaping your desires, motives, thoughts, and actions. Let God search you and lead you in the everlasting way. Download this morning prayer; it will bring vibrancy, help, and hope to your day.

Unstoppablegospel.com/search

Chapter 10

UNSTOPPABLE OBEDIENCE

Leaving the town of McGrath felt tougher than it should have. There was no moon, no silver wash of light across the trail, only a low ceiling of cloud cover pressing down on the Alaskan wilderness and swallowing everything beyond the narrow beam of my headlamp. The cold carried a steady bite, as if it were testing whether I truly belonged out there.

We were 311 miles into the Iditarod Trail Race, and the team was moving fairly well. You learn to feel that as much as you see it, through the rhythm of the dogs, the glide of the sled, and the feedback coming up through the runners on the trail. Still, something was off. Our movement was steady, but the trail beneath us did not feel right.

The snow under the runners was softer than it should have been, lacking the firm, packed base that normally comes from heavy snow machine traffic. It was not terrible, but it was not right, and in a race like the Iditarod, that distinction matters. I lifted my head and swept the darkness with my light, and that was when I saw it. Just twenty feet to our right was the real trail, firm, defined, and properly packed, the path we were meant to be on.

A GROWING READINESS TO RESPOND

Up front was King, my lead dog, strong, athletic, and exceptionally gifted. In many ways, he was the most naturally talented dog on the team. However, like many gifted leaders, King sometimes trusted his own read a little too much, and in this moment, he believed he knew the way.

I gave the command, "Gee, King. Gee," but he did not respond. He continued forward on the softer, parallel trail with confidence and commitment. I called again, "Gee, King. Gee." He continued straight ahead. I tapped the brake and brought the sled to a stop as the team settled and steam rose into the cold night air. Leaning forward, I fixed my eyes on him and gave the command again, "Gee, King. Gee." For a moment, it seemed like he would obey, but when I released the brake, he continued on the same path.

I kept calling to him, not with anger but with urgency. "Gee, King. King, gee." Right behind him were the swing dogs, both named White Eyes. They were not the most gifted, but they were tough, resilient, and increasingly responsive to my voice. As I called out, they began to look back over their shoulders as if asking whether they should step in.

I gave the command again, "Okay, gee," and they responded immediately. They leaned hard to the right, cutting into deep powder and resisting both the pull of the team behind them and the stubborn momentum of the leader in front of them. The move was not smooth, but it was right. Within moments, King felt the power shift, hesitated, adjusted, and then jumped in as the team moved through the soft snow and onto the real Iditarod Trail.

The difference was immediate. The sled ran more smoothly, the pull became more efficient, and the team settled into a stronger rhythm. It was better for the team and better for King, and in that quiet moment under a dark Alaskan sky, it felt as though he understood.

We often live the same way, trusting our instincts and continuing down paths that feel right even when something beneath them is off. When God speaks, we hesitate, not always out of rebellion, but out of confidence in our own understanding. Yet God's vantage point is never limited. He sees what we cannot see and knows the condition of the path beneath us and the struggle it will become if we stay on it.

When He calls us to adjust or make a move, it is not to restrict us but to realign us, and every time we respond, something beneath us and ahead of us has changed. It is not always faster running, but it is always better running. With His will is greater stability, clearer direction, and alignment. That is the beginning of unstoppable obedience, a growing readiness to respond when He speaks and a deepening trust that His way leads to what is best.

Obedience has been badly abused in the church, so let me be clear: It is not a checklist for earning favor with God, nor is it a set of behavior standards to control or judge others. Obedience is about love. It is the gentle voice of God using the Word of God to shape us like clay on a potter's wheel. Bit by bit, He changes us as we submit to Him—and by His grace, and His grace alone, we obey.

THE VOICE

My Bible college and seminary training emphasized systematic theology, the sufficiency of Christ, and the authority of Scripture. We studied the Holy Spirit, wrote doctrinal positions, and affirmed His role theologically. Yet, for all that clarity, something remained untapped. It is possible to affirm the doctrine of the Spirit and still miss the voice of the Spirit and neglect the very "advantage" that Jesus promised, costing us more than we imagine.

> The question is not whether the Spirit speaks, but whether we have learned to recognize His voice.

Much of the New Testament's corrective language about the Spirit appears in 1 Corinthians, where misuse required instruction and a call for restraint. However, the most formative teaching on the Spirit's active role in the believer's life is found elsewhere. In John 14 and John 16, Jesus describes the Spirit not as an abstract force, but as a personal presence. In Romans 8, the Spirit is referenced repeatedly—twenty-two times—within a chapter that begins with the declaration, "There is therefore now no condemnation for those who are in Christ Jesus. For the law of the Spirit of life has set you free in Christ Jesus from the law of sin and death" (Rom. 8:1–2). Freedom, it turns out, is deeply connected to the ongoing work and presence of the Spirit.

Jesus said it was to our advantage that He would go, so that the Holy Spirit would come (John 16:7). That statement demands attention. What is this advantage? What have we been given that we might be neglecting? In His own words, Jesus describes the Spirit as Comforter, Guide, and the One who convicts. He is our Helper (John 14:16–17), with all that implies. He guides us into all truth (John 16:13), and guidance requires someone who speaks and someone who listens for direction. He convicts the world concerning sin, righteousness, and judgment (John 16:8), and conviction presumes a voice that presses truth into the heart, going beyond the noise of self-justification and satanic deception. Jesus also said, "He will teach you all things and bring to your remembrance all that I have said to you" (John 14:26). Remembrance is not mechanical; it is personal. It is the Spirit actively bringing truth to mind at the right moment.

The question, then, is not whether the Spirit speaks, but whether we have learned to recognize His voice. Many have experienced it without naming it. We call them promptings, nudges, impressions, or a deep sense of a word from God. We feel compelled to act, to stop, to speak, or to repent, yet we hesitate to say plainly that the Spirit of God is speaking. However, that is precisely what Scripture affirms.

> Hearing the Spirit's voice is to walk not alone, but led, not guessing, but guided, not merely informed, but transformed.

The great voices of the church have recognized this for generations. John Owen wrote, "The Holy Ghost is the immediate efficient cause of all holiness and obedience in believers."[1] Without the Spirit's active direction, obedience is reduced to human effort. Owen understood that the Spirit is not distant or silent, but present and active, leading the believer in real time.

There is, of course, a caution that must be made. Some fear that an emphasis on listening to the voice of God will lead to confusion or error. That fear, while understandable, is ultimately misplaced when properly grounded. The Word of God remains the final authority and the unchanging standard of truth. The Spirit never contradicts the Scriptures He breathed out. If what we sense leads us away from the Word, it is not the voice of the Spirit, but a spirit with satanic origins. However, when the Spirit speaks, He most often does so by bringing Scripture to mind, illuminating truth, and applying the words of Jesus directly to our lives.

The voice of the Spirit is not given to make life easier, nor to smooth every path before us. It is given to align us with the will of God, to guide us onto paths of righteousness, and to lead us into life as it was meant to be lived. It is the very advantage Jesus promised, how we experience not only direction, but intimacy with God Himself.

To ignore that voice is not lessening our walk with God; it is a crushing loss. It leaves us relying on our own instincts, navigating by limited sight, and missing the very guidance that was meant to shape every step. However, to listen, to recognize, and to respond is to step into the fullness of what has been given. It is to not walk alone, but led, not guessing, but guided, not merely informed, but transformed.

LIKE A ROCK

In a world obsessed with quick fixes and instant results, most people are building their lives on whatever feels stable in the moment. But pressure has a way of exposing what was never truly solid.

In Matthew 7:24–27, Jesus lays out a picture that is as striking as it is simple. He compares two kinds of people who hear the same message, live in the same region, and face the same storms. The rain falls on both. The winds beat against both houses. The floods rise against both foundations. The external conditions are identical, the pressures are equal, and the environment is shared, yet the outcomes are radically different. When the storm comes against the house built on sand, it collapses, and great is its fall. When the storm comes against the house built on the rock, it stands.

> The real issue is not whether we are hearing the voice of God, but whether we are willing to obey the voice of God.

The question we have to ask is what makes the difference. Jesus answers it with one word: obedience. Everyone in the story hears the truth, but that is not the distinction. The distinction is that one applies the truth and the other does not. One builds strength through the application to their life of what he hears, and the other walks away, knowing plenty, applying nothing, and is ultimately unchanged.

We are living in an age of information brokering, and it has subtly reshaped how we think about discipleship. In many ways, we have reduced spiritual growth to the accumulation of knowledge, assuming that if we know more, we will live differently. However, if information alone produced transformation, then the most knowledgeable people on earth would be the most spiritually alive. That was not true in Jesus' day with the Pharisees, and it is not true in ours. The amount of knowledge you possess does not determine the quality of your life; obedience does.

I was sitting with a few friends one day and knew I needed to call David Nelms. David is the founder of the Timothy Initiative, and last year alone they planted over 45,000 churches around the globe, most of them in very difficult areas with a huge cost attached to becoming a disciple of Christ. When he picked up, I said, "I've got one question, David. What's the difference between believers who are thriving in some of the hardest places on earth and those of us with every resource at our fingertips?" He did not hesitate. "That's easy," he said. "One word. Obedience."

That is the dividing line. David went on to make it clear that the real issue is not whether we are hearing the voice of God, but whether we are willing to obey the voice of God. This is deeply personal. It is a below-the-waterline issue. It is not about exposure to truth but response to truth. It is not about knowing more but doing what we already know.

Scripture reinforces this again and again. "But be doers of the word, and not hearers only, deceiving yourselves" (James 1:22). Jesus Himself said, "If you love me, you will keep my commandments" (John 14:15), and then tied that obedience directly to the work of the Spirit, promising the Helper who would empower and guide that very response (John 14:16–17). Obedience is never detached from the Spirit; it is enabled by Him.

J. I. Packer teaches that walking by the Spirit involves responding to the Spirit's guidance as he applies the Word of God to the believer's mind and conscience.[2] That is where power is found, not in accumulation, but in application.

So how do we step into unstoppable obedience? The answer is not found in reading through the Bible in a year, adopting a high-intensity plan, or even increasing church attendance and taking more notes, as valuable as those things can be. The shift is more fundamental than that. It is that our approach to truth becomes radically different starting today. We no longer measure success by how much we know, but by how quickly and faithfully we obey.

BUILT TO LAST

If you were to look at my life over the last couple of years, you might not see dramatic change. Those closest to me would see it, and my wife certainly has, but from a distance it may not look all that different. But if you were to ask people who knew me forty years ago whether my life has changed, most of them would tell you it is unrecognizable. They might call it strange. They might call it extreme. But they would all agree on one thing: It has definitely changed. The real question is how did that happen?

> God wants to set our lives on the rock through simple, repeated acts of obedience.

We tend to overcomplicate the answer. We treat transformation like a mystery when God has made it remarkably clear: It is hearing and applying the Word of God, one truth at a time, over and over again. That's it. That is the unseen thing that matters a lot.

There were moments early on when God moved with stunning speed—miraculous deliverance. He broke a raging cocaine and alcohol addiction in a matter of days. It was decisive and unmistakable. But what followed was not instant perfection. There were face plants and hard lessons. I was a poor husband in our first two years of marriage, and even now, I am still growing. I also made unwise decisions, especially in leadership, getting out in front of God and assuming I knew the way. I had to learn, often the hard way, what it means to walk in wisdom, listen more carefully, and obey more consistently. Yet through all of it, the trajectory changed. Those who knew me decades ago would not debate that. And I credit that entirely to the grace of God.

As we saw earlier in Titus 2:11–12, "The grace of God has appeared . . . training us to renounce ungodliness and worldly passions, and to live self-controlled, upright, and godly lives in the present age." This is training grace. It is not passive. It is active. It is God's power at work in us, shaping us through repeated, applied obedience. Grace teaches. Grace trains. Grace gives us the power to obey. Grace leads.

Anyone who has ever trained for anything understands this. Information alone does not change performance. I was a hurdler in high school, and my trail leg was slow. I spent too much time in the air. My coach could tell me that all day long, but until I practiced and applied that correction, nothing changed. The gap between knowing and doing kept me in the air too long and slowed me down.

Spiritually, many of us live the same way. We are up in the air, hearing the truth but not landing it. What God is after is firm footing. He wants to set our lives on the rock through simple, repeated acts of obedience.

This is the hidden work. This is below the waterline, where real transformation happens. In my own day planner, I keep a column not just for Scripture read, but for truth applied. I do not believe we should ever go to church, open the Bible, or listen to a message without asking, "God, what truth needs to be applied to my life today?" That question changes everything.

It may feel overwhelming at first. You may even take in less information because you are focused on applying what you already know. But over time, something powerful happens. A habit loop forms. Obedience begins to take root. Life starts to align. These are not flashy changes. They are quiet adjustments, like learning to love your spouse sacrificially, becoming slow to speak and quick to listen, putting sin to death with Spirit-endowed power, and walking in step with the Spirit so that the pull of the flesh loses its grip.

So here is a counterintuitive path forward. First, come humbly before God in every learning environment with one commitment: "I will listen for one thing I can apply today." Whether you are reading Scripture or sitting under teaching, posture your heart to hear the voice of the Spirit, and trust that He will guide you.

Second, write it down. Capture it in a journal, a note, or a voice memo. Do not walk away and forget, like the one described in James 1 who looks in a mirror and forgets what he has seen.

Third, bring in one person. Share what God is calling you to apply. This introduces encouragement and accountability at a deeper level. When someone else knows, it strengthens your follow-through and models obedience for others.

Fourth, begin to observe or even journal what God is doing as you align your life with Him. Record the lessons or mark them in your mind, the adjustments, and the evidence of His work. This builds awareness and gratitude.

Fifth, keep listening to the voice of the Spirit. He will continue to remind you of what He has already shown you. This is not limited to a quiet time. You do not just meet with God and then move on with your day. By the power of the Spirit, He walks with you continually, speaking, prompting, correcting, and guiding moment by moment.

God is still changing me to this day. There are still patterns He is refining, still areas where He is sharpening how I think, how I decide, and how I love my wife. Now, as a more seasoned pastor, I also sense a growing call to pass on what I have learned. That calling strengthens me as well, because to carry that baton, to be a torchbearer for others, requires that I continue to walk in the same obedience I am calling others into. All of this is hearing His gentle voice urging me to get aligned with His will and on a path that is much better for traveling.

If I stop applying what God shows me, I do not just stall; I miss out on the very life He is offering. But if you begin today, letting God examine your life, obeying the Word of God like you never have before, one truth at a time, consistently and intentionally, you will be astonished at what God will do.

Built on the Rock

Transformation happens when truth is obeyed. Learn how to put truth into practice before that moment of conviction fades. Watch my conversation with Colin Smith about the power of learning and applying the Word of God to your life.

Unstoppablegospel.com/obey

Chapter 11

UNSTOPPABLE WEAKNESS

Several years ago on a trip to Bermuda, I got a bright idea. Having spent eight seasons commercial fishing in Alaska, I rented a Boston Whaler and decided to take my wife on the adventure of a lifetime.

The day was gorgeous. The sun was shining. Blue skies. Everything looked perfect. What I didn't know was how big the swells were once you got out into open water. The farther we got from shore, the bigger they seemed to get. The Boston Whaler is a seaworthy boat, but I remember thinking, "We're in really big seas in a little boat. This is dicey!"

I never told Junanne what I was feeling that day, but there were a couple of moments that got my full attention. I started reaching back to everything I knew about being on the water and came to one conclusion: We should probably head back.

It's amazing what happens when you realize how small you are. Out there, surrounded by water, I found myself very aware of God—His power, His providence, and how much I needed Him. By the time we got back into the harbor, I was relieved and humbled.

Consider this: The waters we avoid are often the very waters God is calling us into. The place we resist, recoil from, and refuse to enter is often the place where His power is waiting to meet us—where what feels like drowning becomes the very place we are rescued.

The crushing effect on my soul left me so hollow that even now, I struggle to put words to it. What I fought against—what I tried to outrun—was a gnawing emptiness no rush could satisfy and no numbing could silence. Cocaine couldn't fill it. Alcohol couldn't dull it. The deeper the ache, the harder I ran. And yet, the very place I resisted became the place God used to do the impossible. It is in those crushing moments of weakness—those seasons when everything in you collapses—that you begin to see what is actually true: The greatest place you could ever be is not strong, but weak, because it is there that His power breaks in. "For my power is made perfect in weakness" (2 Cor. 12:9).

MARKERS

When I look back over my life, I can trace these moments like markers—places I once called low points but now recognize as holy ground. I think of arriving in Denver, Colorado, stepping into a full schedule at seminary with a calling on my life but little money in my pocket, and not enough hours in the day to make more. A wife and two young children at home, and no clear way to provide. So I got up at 3:00 a.m. in the dead of winter to shovel sidewalks in the dark, pushing through snowstorms with cold hands and a tired body, feeling the weight of it all. Scraping out a living and a life, being the man Dad raised me to be but feeling my inadequacy as I tried to hold it all together. And yet, it was there, in the cold and in the dark, with responsibility pressing in and little strength of my own to rely on, that God met me. Not in what I could do, but in what I could not. Not in my strength, but in my weakness.

I think of the moment my bride, with honesty and pain, shared that her feelings of love for me had gone. That moment exposed me. It revealed what I could not manufacture, what I could not fix, what I could not force. I could not love her on my own the way she deserved, and it was there, in that breaking, that God began to show me a deeper love, His love, flowing through weakness rather than strength.

There were moments of betrayal, blindsides that left me drained, breathless, unable to regain footing—times when I felt completely emptied out, with nothing left emotionally, mentally, or spiritually. And yet it was there that the quiet truth surfaced again: In my weakness, He is strong. Even raising children will take you there, bringing you to the end of yourself where you realize you don't have what it takes, and that realization, as terrifying as it feels, becomes an invitation, because out of that "nothing," God begins to form something entirely different—a strength that is not self-made, but Spirit-given.

These moments of weakness that we've tried to resist, medicate, escape, or even ask God to take away may in fact be one of the greatest graces in our lives—the very places where the gospel becomes unstoppable in us. The weakness we feel when the marriage is strained and we don't know how to fix it, when our body is failing and we can't control it, when anxiety grips us and won't let go, when depression clouds everything, when temptation feels relentless, when we're exhausted and burned out, when finances tighten and fear rises, when relationships fracture, when betrayal cuts deep, when we feel inadequate as parents, when we're overwhelmed at work, when we're battling hidden sin, when we feel spiritually dry, when prayers seem unanswered, when grief lingers longer than we expected, when we're misunderstood, overlooked, or rejected, when we simply don't have the strength to keep going—these are not interruptions to God's work; they are often the very means of it.

Jesus spoke a truth that embodies every unclimbable mountain and every uncrossable river: "With man this is impossible, but with God all things are possible" (Matt. 19:26). And I can say it now with experiential clarity, the moments I thought would break me were the moments that built me. "For when I am weak, then I am strong" (2 Cor. 12:10).

WEAKNESS ALL AROUND

Habakkuk was a prophet of God, likely ministering in Judah around 605 BC, just before the Babylonian invasion. He stood at a fault line in history as Assyria collapsed and Babylon rose, with everything familiar beginning to give way. He wasn't observing this from a distance; he was living in it, watching his nation erode from within while a storm gathered on the horizon.

He lived in a world that feels uncomfortably close to ours—violent, corrupt, morally inverted, and spiritually numb. What was wrong had become normal, and what was right was being pushed aside. Leadership was compromised, justice was twisted, and truth had lost its footing. When Habakkuk looked out, it didn't just concern him; it rocked him. "Violence!" he cried, not as exaggeration, but as reality. Destruction, strife, and contention were everywhere. "The wicked surround the righteous." The law had stalled out, and justice no longer landed where it should (Hab. 1:2–4). The weight of it all wasn't just scary, it was weakening.

The pressure point wasn't only what he saw, but what he couldn't reconcile. How does a holy God allow this? How long does this go on? Why does it feel like heaven is silent while everything on earth is unraveling? This was a man feeling the world close in on him, realizing he didn't have the strength to make sense of it, let alone fix it.

Then God answered, but not in a way that relieved the tension. God said He was raising up the Chaldeans, a ruthless empire, feared and relentless, sweeping through nations and devouring everything in their path (Hab. 1:5–11). That answer didn't steady Habakkuk; it shook him further. Now the problem was bigger. How could God use something more corrupt to deal with what was already corrupt? How could the wicked swallow up those more righteous while God appeared to hold back (Hab. 1:12–17)?

This is weakness pressing in from the outside—the kind that comes from what you see, what you're facing, and what you can't control. A world unraveling. Pressure mounting. Questions unanswered. It leaves you feeling small, overwhelmed, and outmatched.

We know that feeling. When you look around and see the same patterns—confusion, compromise, injustice—it drains you. In that moment, two instincts rise up. One is to shut down. The other is to power up—to push harder, speak sharper, and try to force things into place. That second instinct is where danger creeps in. It produces an angry Christianity—reactive, brittle, fueled by frustration more than trust. It looks strong, but it isn't. It's weakness trying to pass itself off as strength.

Habakkuk doesn't go there. He doesn't numb out, and he doesn't lash out. He steps into the tension and stays there before God. "I will take my stand at my watchpost . . . and look out to see what he will say to me" (Hab. 2:1). There is no pretending and no posturing—just a man bringing his weakness, the weight of the world pressing in, into the presence of God and waiting there. That's the turn. Strength doesn't begin when you gather yourself; it begins when you release yourself to God.

By the time you reach the end of Habakkuk, nothing has improved externally. The threat remains, the loss is still coming, and the collapse he feared hasn't been removed. Yet he says,

> Though the fig tree should not blossom, nor fruit be on the vines . . . yet I will rejoice in the Lord; I will take joy in the God of my salvation. God, the Lord, is my strength. (Hab. 3:17–19)

The world around him is still unstable, but he is no longer anchored to it. His strength has shifted. Habakkuk now demonstrated a stubborn confidence in God that refused to be dictated by circumstances. Even when the fields were barren, the flocks were gone, and every visible sign of provision had disappeared, he chose to rejoice in the Lord and trust that God would be enough.

Then you come to Paul, and the direction of weakness changes. Habakkuk felt weakness from the outside—what was happening around him. Paul felt it from the inside—what was happening within him. He speaks of a "thorn in the flesh," something that would not leave him, something that kept him dependent and exposed his limits. He tells us plainly, "Three times I pleaded with the Lord about this, that it should leave me" (2 Cor. 12:8). He asked for relief. He asked God to take it away, and the answer was no.

> Weakness is not something to escape; it is the place where God meets you.

Instead, God said, "My grace is sufficient for you, for my power is made perfect in weakness" (v. 9). So Paul concludes, "For the sake of Christ, then, I am content with weaknesses, insults, hardships, persecutions, and calamities. For when I am weak, then I am strong" (v. 10).

Do you see it? Two directions of weakness. Habakkuk faced the weight of a broken world pressing in from the outside. Paul carried the reality of personal limitation rising from the inside. One is the pressure of circumstances; the other is the pressure of condition. Both become the exact place where God meets them.

Weakness is not something to escape; it is the place where God meets you. Whether it's what's happening around you that you cannot control or what's happening within you that you cannot overcome, both are invitations. Both are where His power shows up.

We spend much of our lives trying to eliminate weakness—manage it, outrun it, cover it up, compensate for it. But both Habakkuk and Paul show us the same truth: The very place we try to avoid is the place where God is waiting. The pressure from the outside and the limitation on the inside are not barriers; they are doorways.

Habakkuk stood under the weight of a collapsing world and found that God was his strength. Paul stood in the reality of his own limitation and found that Christ's power rested on him. Different pressures, same meeting place.

And that's where we are brought—not to a place where we finally become strong enough, but to a place where we stop trying to be. It is right there, when the world is too much and you are not enough, that God does what only He can do. "For when I am weak, then I am strong."

HUMBLE AND UNOFFENDABLE

"You look pretty rough, Pastor!" Normally a comment like that would have deflated me. I guess this brother was just calling it as he saw it. And I probably didn't look good. The night before I had pitched the message I was going to give the next morning at church. I was without a word and now only twelve hours until I was to preach. Nothing was on paper or in my heart. But in my weakness God met me in power. I was so lacking in anything that I was laid bare and asking God to pull off a miracle. In my weakness, I was so reliant on God to show up that I was emptied of self, humbled to my core, and utterly dependent on God to come through. He did it! My connection with God in my weakness was so profound that I was impervious to the "you look pretty rough" dig, as I was about to give His message.

If you resolve to embrace your weakness, you will find this powerful virtue come to life in you: humility. Many have tried to explain what humility looks like, but it's best seen in relationships. When someone bumps your cup you can see what spills out. Humility, true humility, gives birth to the superpower of being unoffendable. Even saying that feels unrealistic. The idea of being truly unoffendable sounds like something reserved for the strong. But Scripture—and experience—pushes us somewhere deeper. When our weakness is embraced, when it fills the heart so completely that it crowds out every corner where we pretended we were strong, something remarkable begins to grow. The fruit of that kind of posture is not earthly weakness, but a settled, Spirit-formed strength that simply cannot be easily offended.

> It was a graphic contrast: pride dressed up as piety on one side, and quiet, costly surrender on the other.

One little known picture of this "unoffendability" is the woman with two copper coins. Jesus is sitting opposite the treasury, watching the crowd put money into the offering boxes. Wealthy contributors are making a show of their giving, large sums clinking loudly into trumpet-shaped receptacles designed so that everyone could hear and take notice. And then, almost unnoticed, a widow makes her way forward—no entourage, no attention, no status—her two copper coins likely barely making a tinkle as they fall in. She steps into a system she knows is broken, surrounded by religious pride and public display, and still, she moves forward in quiet, resolute trust.

"She out of her poverty has put in everything she had, all she had to live on" (Mark 12:44). What she gives is materially insignificant, but spiritually massive. No comparison. No calculation. No hesitation rooted in what others are doing or not doing. Just surrender. And then Jesus calls His disciples and reframes everything: "Truly, I say to you, this poor widow has put in more than all those who are contributing to the offering box" (Mark 12:43).

Just moments earlier, Jesus had warned about the scribes who "devour widows' houses" (Mark 12:40), and now there was living evidence of a system that burdened the vulnerable while rewarding appearances. This same temple system is what He had already confronted in explosive fashion when He overturned the tables of the

> Humility starts with a choice—to release your right to be right, heard, vindicated.

money changers (Mark 11:15–17), declaring that they had turned His Father's house into a den of robbers. So when Jesus looked up and saw that widow, He was not simply observing generosity—He was seeing through a corrupt religious culture into the raw, unfiltered reality of the human heart. It was graphic in its contrast: pride dressed up as piety on one side, and quiet, sweetly embraced weakness on the other. And without hesitation, Jesus honored what the world would overlook and exposed what the world would celebrate.

The widow could have hung back and not risked her meager offering being compared with others' large amounts. She would have been justified in feeling offended by their bravado. She could have neglected giving at all. But in her weakness she was strong. The widow embraced weakness, found strength in God, and it made her humble and unoffendable.

Brant Hansen captures humility in a unique and powerful way: "We should forfeit our right to be offended. That means forfeiting our right to hold on to anger. When we do this, we'll be making a sacrifice that's very pleasing to God. It strikes at our very pride. It forces us not only to think about humility, but to actually be humble."[1] That's not pretending wrong doesn't happen or injustice isn't real. But it's becoming the kind of person who is no longer ruled by it.

We often mischaracterize weakness and humility. We attach it to personality types—quiet people, soft-spoken people, externally gentle people. But those traits, while sometimes accompanying humility, are not humility itself. You can be outwardly calm and internally raging with self-reliance. You can speak little and still be consumed with self. The fruit of humility is far more revealing, and one of its clearest expressions is the growing ability to be unoffendable.

But this is not natural. This kind of humility does not emerge in comfort—it is cultivated in quiet places with God. And yet, there is something astonishing about it. While humility is supernatural in its formation, it is profoundly practical in its beginning. It starts with a choice. Not a personality trait, not a family vibe, not even a spiritual gift selectively given, but a decision—to lower yourself, to release your right to be right, to surrender your need to be heard, defended, or vindicated.

Andrew Murray captured this with clarity: "Humility is nothing but the disappearance of self in the vision that God is all."[2] That is the difference. True weakness and humility is not self-focused; it is God-focused. That kind of weakness does not need to be seen, named, or validated. It simply rests in God.

This is what healthy weakness looks like. It is Moses standing before the burning bush saying, "Who am I that I should go?" (Ex. 3:11), not as an excuse to withdraw, but as a confession that drives him into dependence.

It is Gideon admitting he is the least in his family and his clan the weakest in Manasseh, yet stepping forward because God says, "I will be with you" (Judg. 6:15–16).

It is David running toward Goliath, not in self-confidence, but declaring, "The battle is the Lord's" (1 Sam. 17:47).

It is Paul saying, "We have this treasure in jars of clay, to show that the surpassing power belongs to God and not to us" (2 Cor. 4:7).

Scripture never calls us to settle into weakness as an end state. It calls us to move through weakness into dependence so that the power of God can be put on display.

Healthy weakness does not shrink back, and it does not strive forward in the flesh. It moves forward with a settled awareness that any strength that shows up must come from God.

This is what spiritualized weakness looks like. It is Saul offering sacrifices he was never commanded to give because he feared the people and felt the pressure to act (1 Sam. 13:8–12). It is self-reliance dressed up as necessity. It is the Israelites saying they cannot enter the land because the giants are too big, even after God has promised to go before them (Num. 13:31–33). It is unbelief cloaked in realism. It is Peter declaring, "Even if I must die with you, I will not deny you," only to fall hours later because his confidence was in himself (Matt. 26:33–35, 69–75). That is not embracing weakness; that is ignoring it. And when weakness is ignored, it always defaults to pride.

The question rises, then: Is it right to seek the power of God? The answer is a clear yes. Scripture never calls us to settle into weakness as an end state. It calls us to move through weakness into dependence so that the power of God can be put on display. Paul's life makes this unmistakable. "By the grace of God I am what I am," he says, "and his grace toward me was not in vain . . . though it was not I, but the grace of God that is with me" (1 Cor. 15:10). There is effort there, movement. But the source is clear. It is all grace.

And when that settles into the soul, everything begins to shift. We can say with Paul, "I have learned in whatever situation I am, to be content . . . I know how to be brought low, and I know how to abound . . . I can do all things through him who strengthens me" (Phil. 4:11–13). That is not situational strength. That is anchored strength.

Weakness embraced is not something reserved for moments when we are down and out. It is a posture we carry when we are up and out. When we have little, we depend on God. When we have much, we depend on God. In famine, we trust Him. In harvest, we trust Him. In obscurity, we lean in. In influence, we lean in. In suffering, we rely on Him. In success, we rely on Him. When doors close, we trust His hand. When doors open, we trust His heart. At every level, in every season, we recognize that apart from Him we have nothing, and in Him we have everything.

Hudson Taylor is remembered for saying, "All God's giants have been weak men who did great things for God because they reckoned on God being with them."[3] That is the tension held rightly. We are not passive, but we are not self-powered. We move, but we move in dependence. We act, but we act in surrender.

Weakness is not the goal. Dependence is. And weakness, when it is real, when it is embraced, when it is brought honestly before God, becomes the doorway through which His power is made known.

DEEPER STILL

There are many spiritual disciplines to be realized in the walk of faith. To use your spiritual gifts—as a leader, administrator, teacher, encourager, giver, one who shows mercy—these are profound. They are deeply meaningful, deeply impactful, and deeply beneficial to the people around you. They build up the body. They strengthen the church. They matter. These are above the waterline.

They're necessary. But what they're born of, where they germinate, how they grow, matters most. And unleashing the power of God is tapped somewhere deeper still.

And to see it, we must see a vision of the person of Christ Jesus. We are, after all, apprentices of Him. In Philippians 2, Paul calls us into a mindset that runs completely counter to the instincts of the flesh:

> Do nothing from selfish ambition or conceit, but in humility count others more significant than yourselves. Let each of you look not only to his own interests, but also to the interests of others. Have this mind among yourselves, which is yours in Christ Jesus. (Phil. 2:3–5)

The word Paul uses for "humility" is the Greek *tapeinophrosynē*. It is formed from *tapeinos*, meaning lowly or brought low, and *phroneō*, meaning to set one's mind, to direct one's thinking. This is not a passing feeling or a personality trait; it is a disciplined way of thinking—a settled, chosen mindset that moves downward, that willingly takes the lower place.

This discipline is a final emptying of oneself—*kenosis*. It is the realization that all that we are and all that we do is by the grace of God alone, both in the "big" moments and in the quiet, steady dailiness of life.

Living in this broken and fallen world, there is a quiet assumption that no one can remain there consistently—that this kind of life is reserved for moments, not a manner of living. But holiness and training in righteousness call us deeper still. They call us to live there more and more, to grow in consistency, to renounce our need for control, our craving for recognition, our subtle grasp for credit, and to return again and again to dependence on God.

When we go deeper still—when we allow God to strip away what we cling to and expose what we trust in—we begin to experience a life that is no longer driven by self-effort but sustained by divine grace. We are no longer striving to prove anything. We are no longer grasping for position or validation. We are no longer trying to generate something that only God can give. We have nothing to prove, nothing to grasp, and everything to receive.

The gospel becomes unstoppable in the lives of those who cultivate, in the unseen places, a heart fully yielded to God—a heart alive to His providence, anchored in His goodness, resting in His grace, and shaped by His mercy. From that place, life begins to flow—not manufactured, not forced, but carried along by the power of God Himself.

Take this journey, friend, because it is through vessels like this—emptied, yielded, dependent—that the gospel of Jesus Christ moves with unstoppable power.

Your Weakness Is Your Strength

Weakness is the catalyst to be powerfully used by God. Watch my conversation with Susie Larson on the power of weakness. Like many, Susie has gone through significant hardship physically, relationally, and spiritually. Let her story encourage you.

Unstoppablegospel.com/weak

YOUR NEXT STEP

The Unstoppable Gospel truly changes everything! You are now armed with truth that clarifies the path ahead and you now have a greater vision for yourself and others. Continue becoming the kind of disciple Jesus intended. I want to help . . .

Say NO to self-help and YES to God's power.

Many genuine disciples of Christ have grown accustomed to bad habits, written off lifelong battles as unwinnable, or believed that some destructive behaviors can never be altered. *The 7 Resolutions* is for you.

This book, with accompanying study guides, and assessments will teach you how to overthrow old patterns, create new life systems, and take hold of God's promises. Resolve to:

- Join God
- Think Truth
- Kill Sin
- Choose Friends
- Take Risks
- Focus Effort
- Redeem Time

Never settle for too little. The time is now for humble dependence on God and a plan to walk in His power. It's time to come alive!

Unstoppablegospel.com/seven

ACKNOWLEDGMENTS

God has been so good to me, and this project would never have gotten off the ground without a few key people.

Randy Hall, thank you for lending me a title that fits my heart and passion to a T.

Drew Dyck, you are one of the most skilled editors and personal encouragers I have ever known.

Pam Pugh, your keen eye and willingness to examine a manuscript with such granularity have been invaluable.

Lori Ridder, my executive assistant, you not only keep the trains running on time; you lighten my load and make efforts like this possible.

Christianne Debysingh, thank you for bringing your skill, wisdom, and enthusiasm as a publicist to this project. Your ability to help this message find its audience has been an invaluable gift.

Erica Dvorak, your energy and passion for getting the gospel to market are second to none. Thank you for believing so deeply in this message and working tirelessly to help it reach as many people as possible.

Junanne Clauson, you are my best friend, toughest editor, and the greatest asset in my life.

Finally, how could I write an acknowledgment without recognizing the grace of God? I have experienced His favor and power as He has deepened my passion for this message. If this book bears any fruit, the glory goes to Him alone.

NOTES

Chapter 1: How We Deserted God

1. Dean Inserra, *The Unsaved Christian: Reaching Cultural Christianity with the Gospel* (Moody Publishers, 2019).
2. In Christianity, specifically within evangelicalism and revivalism, decisionism refers to the belief that an individual is saved the moment they perform an external act of "deciding" for Christ.
3. Martyn Lloyd-Jones, *Preachers and Preaching* (Zondervan, 1971), 269–79.
4. Dallas Willard, *The Great Omission* (HarperOne, 2006), 3–4.
5. Dallas Willard, *The Divine Conspiracy: Rediscovering Our Hidden Life in God* (HarperSanFrancisco, 1998), 40–41.
6. A. W. Tozer, *I Call It Heresy!* (Moody Publishers, 2010), 18.
7. John Calvin, *Galatians*, on Galatians 1:6, in *Calvin's Commentaries*, vol. 21, trans. William Pringle (Calvin Translation Society, 1844).
8. John R. W. Stott, *The Message of Galatians* (The Bible Speaks Today series) (IVP Academic, 2021), commentary on Galatians 1:6–9.

Chapter 2: How We Deceived a Generation

1. Barna, *2026 American Worldview Inventory* (Barna Institute, 2026).
2. Pew Research, *2023–2024 U. S. Religious Landscape Interactive Database* (Pew Research Center, 2025).
3. Barna, *2026 American Worldview Inventory.*
4. Rogers Commission Report, *House Report 99–1016,* Appendix, 1986.
5. Charles Haddon Spurgeon, "Faith and Repentance Inseparable" (sermon 460, Metropolitan Tabernacle, 1862).
6. J. C. Ryle, "Few Saved!," sermon, 1877.
7. Jonathan Edwards, *A Treatise Concerning Religious Affections* (1746), in *The Works of Jonathan Edwards*, vol. 2, ed. John E. Smith (New Haven: Yale University Press, 1959), Part I, sec. I.

8. Dietrich Bonhoeffer, *The Cost of Discipleship* (Touchstone, 1995), 45–47.

9. Martyn Lloyd-Jones, *God's Ultimate Purpose: An Exposition on Ephesians 1* (Baker Books, 1998).

10. Dallas Willard, attributed teaching of Dallas Willard on trust and obedience in discipleship (often quoted from *The Renovation of the Heart* and lecture materials).

Chapter 3: How We Crippled Disciple-Making

1. Tobin Perry, "Top 20 Countries Where Christianity Is Growing the Fastest," *Global Christian Relief* (Feb. 27, 2025), citing data from the Center for the Study of Global Christianity at Gordon-Conwell Theological Seminary.

2. David Nelms on *Karl and Crew*, circa 2022.

3. Dallas Willard, *The Great Omission* (HarperOne, 2006 edition), xv.

4. Richard Foster, *Celebration of Discipline: The Path to Spiritual Growth* (Harper-SanFrancisco, 1998), 1.

5. Jen Wilkin, *Women of the Word: How to Study the Bible with Both Our Hearts and Our Minds*, 2nd ed. (Crossway, 2019), 27.

Chapter 4: The Curse

1. Timothy Keller, *The Meaning of Marriage: Facing the Complexities of Commitment with the Wisdom of God* (Dutton, 2011), 31.

Chapter 5: The Cure

1. John Calvin, *The Institutes of the Christian Religion*, 1536, Book I, Chapter 1.

2. Alistair Begg, "No Vacancy?," sermon preached at Parkside Church, Chagrin Falls, OH, December 24, 1988, audio available at https://www.truthforlife.org/resources/sermon/no-vacancy/.

3. J. C. Ryle, *Old Paths*, chapter "Conversion," page 182 in the Reformed on the Web PDF edition.

Chapter 6: The With-God Life

1. A. W. Tozer, *The Pursuit of God* (Christian Publications, 1948), 33.

2. John Newton, "Amazing Grace," published in 1779. Public Domain.

3. A. W. Tozer, *The Pursuit of God* (Moody Publishers, 2007), 43.

4. Hudson Taylor, *China's Millions* (Official Writings of China Inland Mission, circa mid 1800s).

5. Richard J. Foster, *Celebration of Discipline: The Path to Spiritual Growth* (HarperSanFrancisco, 1998).

6. Dallas Willard, *The Spirit of the Disciplines: Understanding How God Changes Lives* (HarperCollins, 1988).

Chapter 7: Unstoppable Love

1. Richard Sibbes, *The Bruised Reed* (1630), in *The Works of Richard Sibbes*, ed. Alexander Grosart (Edinburgh: James Nichol, 1862), 1:52.

2. Charles Haddon Spurgeon, "Negotiating with God," Sermon 3433, The Metropolitan Tabernacle Pulpit, 1914.

3. Jerry Bridges, *The Discipline of Grace: God's Role and Our Role in the Pursuit of Holiness* (NavPress, 1994), 19.

4. Martyn Lloyd-Jones, quoted in *Reformation & Revival Journal*, vol. 13, no. 3, 173.

Chapter 8: Unstoppable Surrender

1. Timothy Keller, *Counterfeit Gods: The Empty Promises of Money, Sex, and Power, and the Only Hope That Matters* (Penguin Books, 2011), xix.

Chapter 9: Unstoppable Examination

1. Charles Haddon Spurgeon, *The Treasury of David Vol 3* (Passmore & Alabaster, 1882), commentary on Ps. 139:23–24.

2. Augustine of Hippo, *Soliloquies Book 2*, circa AD 400.

3. Carl Keil and Franz Delitzsch, *Commentary on the Old Testament* (Eerdmans, 1982).

Chapter 10: Unstoppable Obedience

1. John Owen, *Pneumatologia*, Book II, chapter 3.

2. J. I. Packer, *Keep in Step with the Spirit* (Baker Books, rev. ed., 2005), in his treatment of Christian guidance and the role of Scripture in the Spirit's leading.

Chapter 11: Unstoppable Weakness

1. Brant Hansen, *Unoffendable: How Just One Change Can Make All of Life Better* (Thomas Nelson, 2023), 2.

2. Andrew Murray, *Humility: The Beauty of Holiness* (Fleming H. Revell, 1895), Preface.

3. Dr. & Mrs. Howard Taylor, *Hudson Taylor's Spiritual Secret* (Morgan & Scott, various editions). Statement attributed in narrative sections on Taylor's dependence on God; exact wording varies by edition.